SALTY WORDS

BEGOTTEN IN THE GALLEY
AND BORN UNDER A GUN,
EVERY HAIR A ROPE YARN,
EVERY TOOTH A MARLINE SPIKE,
EVERY FINGER A FISHHOOK,
AND ALL OUR HEART'S BLOOD
GOOD STOCKHOLM TAR

SALTY WORDS

Robert Hendrickson

HEARST MARINE BOOKS
NEW YORK 1984

Library of Congress Catalog Card Number: 84-80493

ISBN: 0-688-03550-7

Printed in the United States of America

BOOK DESIGN BY JAMES UDELL

*With all my love
to my daughter Karen*

Introduction

Ahoy might be the best word with which to begin our "sailor's word-book," for *ahoy* is not only a nautical salutation (the word a combination of the interjection *a* and *hoy*, a natural exclamation that is first recorded as a cry for calling hogs, of all things), but it is also a "salty" expression known to millions internationally. So many people are familiar with *ahoy*, in fact, that Alexander Graham Bell suggested it as the salutation for telephone calls when he invented the telephone. The term never caught on, however, because phone users opted for *hello* and deprived *ahoy* of an even more prominent place in the language. In any case, this sailor's wordbook certainly attempts to collect a large, representative sample of the myriad seafaring words and expressions that have so immensely enriched our language. But beyond this it is meant to provide hours of pleasure to everyone with "tar in their heart's blood" or "sand in their shoes" by presenting as many salty words as possible— whether the nautical expressions originated at sea or not.

Most of the following five hundred or so expressions relating to or deriving from the sea and the seafaring life are English in origin, and a good number date back to times when the inhabitants of England were merely a rude painted tribe with no vessel more sophisticated than a burned-out log. For appropriately enough, English nautical terms are mostly Anglo-Saxon or Dutch in origin, quite the opposite of English military terms, which usually have a Norman heritage. Examples would include: *ship, boat, punt, boom, bowsprit, helm, stern, bow, mast, spar, sail, hold, lading, hatchway, rope, tar, hawser, wheel, porthole, keel, tack, ladder, hull, shrouds, dock, rudder, yard, skipper, skiff, mate, sailor, boatswain, coxswain, steward, steersman, crew, luff, thwart, leeward, aft, abaft, taut, deck, reef, ebb, flow, neap, rig, board, knot* and many other words. Yet the sources for nautical terms include practically every language on earth, from across the Channel in France to America, Japan, China, India, the South Seas, and what used to be called darkest Africa. In all these ports every group from pilots to pirates have contributed to the language of the sea. Purely technical terms have been omitted here—they would fill another book—but I have tried to make this an accurate as well as lively account, checking each derivation carefully in as many sources as possible. Nevertheless, no good yarn is omitted just because it's untrue; all such traditional tales are simply labeled as such. I'd like to thank the many people, too numerous to list here, who helped me with this work, especially my wife, Marilyn, who shared in so much of the research, and Paul Larsen, publisher of Hearst Marine Books, who had faith in the project. I hope readers will enjoy the results, and I wish a bon voyage to all those inspired enough to undertake expeditions of their own into the vast ocean of words that constitutes the language of the sea.

—R.H.
Far Rockaway, N.Y.

Let your speech be always with grace,
seasoned with salt.

THE EPISTLE OF PAUL TO THE COLOSSIANS
4:6

AB

AB stands for an *able-bodied seaman*, a first-class sailor who is a skilled seaman, has passed through his training as an *ordinary seaman* and can steer a ship as well as perform all the other work of his rating. The expression *able-bodied* dates back to seventeenth-century England. *Apprentices* or *boys* formed the other class among the crews on early sailing ships.

Adamaster

A fascinating story is told about this ancient sea monster. Vasco da Gama is said to have seen a hideous phantom called the *Adamaster*, the spirit of the stormy Cape of Good Hope, which warned him not to undertake his third voyage to India. Da Gama made the voyage anyway and died soon after reaching his destination.

Admiral

Technically, all *admirals* come from the Arabian desert. The word can be traced to the title of Abu Bakr, who was called *Amir-al-muninin*, commander of the faithful, before he succeeded Mohammed as caliph in A.D. 632. The title *Amir*, or commander, became popular soon after, and naval chiefs were designated *Amir-al-ma*, commander of the water, *Amir-al-bahr*, commander of the sea, and even *Amir-al-amara*, commander of commanders. Western seamen who came in contact with the Arabs assumed that *Amir-al* was one word, and believed this was a distinguished title. By the early thirteenth century, officers were calling themselves *amiral*, which merely means "commander of." The *d* was probably added to the word through a common mispronunciation, although one writer has speculated that the resplendent uniform of some forgotten sea lord might have put it there.

This theory suggests that *admiral* has nothing to do with the Arabs, but that it derives from *admire*, which is from the Latin root "to wonder at," the splendid dress of an unknown naval officer having inspired the word. But *admiral* more probably comes from the title of Abu Bakr, a faithful follower of Mohammed. He is also indirectly honored by the admiral butterfly and admiral sea shell, both as resplendent as that anonymous admiral's uniform. *Admiral Browning* is a personified color, slang for human excrement. And H. L. Mencken observed that there has been at least one honorary *Kentucky Admiral*, an *Admiral of the Kentucky River* who outranked all the Kentucky colonels.

Admiral Cockburn's Letter C

C is probably the highly modified form of an ancient sign for a camel. One of the strangest stories attached to any letter is told about it. It seems that an Admiral George Cockburn led the incendiaries who demolished the *National Intelligencer* when the British burned Washington during the War of 1812. This gentlemanly incendiary ordered his men to melt down all the *C*'s in the newspaper office, "so that later they can't abuse my name."

Aegean Sea

Athenian King Aegeus of Greek mythology gives his name to the Aegean Sea. His son, Theseus, promised to hoist a white sail on his voyage home from Crete, to signal that he was alive. When Theseus neglected to do so, Aegeus, thinking his son had been killed, committed suicide by throwing himself into the sea that came to be named for him.

Afterward

The Saxons called the stern of a boat the *aft*. Their word *ward* meant "in the direction of," so *aftward* meant "toward the rear of a ship," or "behind." Over a long period, the word changed in spelling to *afterward* and came to mean "behind in time," "later on," or "later."

Albatross

The *albatross*, probably the subject of more legends than any other seabird, takes its name from a corruption of the Portuguese *al-catraz*, meaning "large pelican." Also dubbed *gooney birds* because of their clumsy behavior, the big albatrosses—whose wingspans often reach twelve feet, greater than that of any other bird—frequently lumber about the decks of ships, unable to take off after they land because of the cramped space, and actually get as seasick as any landlubber. Sailors have actually hooked them out of the air on baited lines. Another name for them is *mollymawks* or *mol-lyhawks*, from the Dutch *mollemok*, "stupid gulls." Despite their apparent stupidity and stubbornness—nothing can force them to abandon their nesting sites, as the U.S. Navy learned at Midway Island—and their poor flying ability when there is no wind current, albatrosses have managed to thrive.

The many legends about the *Cape Hope sheep* include one claiming they sleep in flight (probably because they are master gliders on the wind) and another holding that they are good-luck omens and that any sailor who kills an albatross will bring disaster to his ship. When the Ancient Mariner shot an albatross with his crossbow in Samuel Taylor Coleridge's "The Rime of the Ancient Mariner," terrible luck followed. It is said that Coleridge based the poem on a true story William Wordsworth told him about privateer George Shelvocke, who shot a black albatross while rounding Cape Horn in 1720 aboard the *Speedwell*.

All at Sea

A feeling of complete helplessness or bewilderment. Most early mariners hugged the coastlines when they voyaged from place to place because their navigational aids were crude and inaccurate. Often however, they were blown far out to sea where they had no landmarks to guide them. The expression *all at sea* described their plight perfectly, as anyone ever caught in rough, open seas will testify, and the term was soon used to describe the condition of any confused, helpless person.

All in the Same Boat

Only a little more than a century old, this saying means that two or more people are sharing the same risks or living under similar conditions. It may derive from some unknown situation when two or more people were adrift in the same lifeboat, or it may even come from the earlier expression *to stick* or *have an oar in another's boat*; that is, to meddle in someone else's affairs, which dates back to the sixteenth century.

All Pooped

If you're *all pooped*, you feel something like the nineteenth-century seamen who used the expression *pooped* to indicate what happened when they were caught on the poop or aft deck of a ship when a wave crashed down and washed over them.

Aloof

To stand aloof was originally a sea term meaning "to bear to windward," or *luff*, which derives from the Dutch *loef*, meaning "windward." Since a ship cannot hold to the windward except by keeping the bow of the ship away from the wind, the term took on the general meaning of "to keep away from," "to keep at a distance," "to be reserved or reticent."

Amazon River

The original *Amazons*, from the Greek *a* (*without*) plus *mazos* (*breast*), were supposedly a tribe of fierce warrior women who cut or burned off their right breasts so as not to impede the drawing of their bows. Any males born from the Amazons' annual union with a neighboring male tribe were either killed or banished. Amazons have been reported in Africa and South America as well as in Greece. The great *Amazon River*, which had previously been named Rio Santa María de la Mar Dulce by its discoverer, is said to have been rechristened the *Amazon* by the Spanish explorer Francisco de Orellana in 1541 after he was attacked by the Tapuyas, a tribe in which he believed women fought alongside men.

Amerigo Vespucci

America, Columbia

Many writers have libelously assumed that the Italian navigator Amerigo Vespucci (whom Ralph Waldo Emerson called "a thief" and "pickle dealer at Seville") was a con man who never explored the New World and doesn't deserve to be mentioned in the same breath as Christopher Columbus, much less have his name honored by the continent. Deeper investigation reveals that Vespucci, born in Florence in 1454, did indeed sail to the New World with the expedition of Alonso de Ojeda in 1499, parting with him even before land was sighted in the West Indies. Vespucci, sailing in his own ship, then discovered and explored the mouth of the Amazon, subsequently sailing along the northern shores of South America. Returning to Spain in 1500, he entered the service of the Portuguese and the following year explored six thousand miles along the southern coast of South America. He was eventually made Spain's pilot major and died at the age of fifty-eight of malaria contracted on his voyages.

Vespucci not only explored unknown regions but also invented a system of computing exact longitude and arrived at a figure computing the earth's equational circumference only fifty miles short of the correct measurement. It was, however, not his many solid accomplishments but a mistake made by a German map maker that led to America being named after him—and this is probably why his reputation suffers even today. Vespucci (who had Latinized his name to Americus Vespucci) wrote many letters about his voyages, including one to the notorious Italian ruler Lorenzo de' Medici in which he described "the New World." But several of his letters were rewritten and sensationalized by an unknown author, who published these forgeries as *Four Voyages* in 1507. One of the forged letters was read by the brilliant young German cartographer Martin Waldseemüller, who was so impressed with Vespucci's account that he included a map of the New World in an appendix to his book *Cosmographiae Introductio,* boldly labeling the land "America." Wrote Waldseemüller in his Latin text, which also included the forged letter: "By now, since these parts have been more extensively explored and another 4th part has been discovered by Americus Vespucius (as will appear from what follows); I see no reason why it should not be called Amerigo, after Americus, the discoverer, or indeed America, since both Europe and Asia have a feminine form from the names of women."

Waldseemüller's map roughly represented South America and when cartographers finally added North America, they retained the original name; the great geographer Gerhardus Mercator finally gave the name America to all of the Western Hemisphere. Vespucci never tried to have the New World named after him or to belittle his friend Columbus, who once called him "a very worthy man." The appellation *America* gained in usage because Columbus refused all his life to admit that he had discovered a new continent, wanting instead to believe that he had come upon an unexplored region in Asia. Spain stubbornly refused to call the New World anything but Columbia until the eighteenth century, but to no avail. Today Columbus is credited for his linguistic precedence only in story and song ("Columbia, the Gem of the Ocean"), while Amerigo Vespucci is honored by hundreds of words ranging from *American know-how* to *American cheese*. The one copy of the *Hauslab-Liechtenstein World Global Map* on which Waldseemüller noted Vespucci's name went up for sale at auction in 1950, but there were no takers at the starting price of fifty thousand dollars.

The America's Cup

The America's Cup

Not the *American Cup* or the *Americus Cup*. This racing trophy was originally called the Hundred Guinea Cup when it was offered by the Royal Yacht Squadron to the winner of an international yacht race around the Isle of Wight. The U.S. schooner *America* won the first race in 1875, defeating fourteen British yachts, and the cup, still a great prize in yachting today, was renamed in her honor. Since that time nearly $100 million has been spent by yachtsmen trying to win the trophy, which is now presented to the winner of a series of races for 12-meter yachts. American yachts won the cup in every competition until 1983, when the Australians took it home to Perth, ending the longest winning streak in sports.

Anadama Bread

Anadama bread, a Yankee cornmeal recipe, offers one of the most humorous stories connected with an eponymous foodstuff. Tradition has it that a Yankee fisherman, whose wife, Anna, was too lazy to cook for him, invented the recipe. On tasting the result of his efforts, a neighbor asked him what he called the bread. The crusty Yankee replied, "Anna, damn her!"

Another version claims that the husband was a Yankee sea captain who endearingly referred to his wife as "Anna, damn 'er." Anna's bread was much loved by his crew because it was both delicious and would not spoil on long sea voyages. The captain is said to have written the following epitaph for his wife: *"Anna was a lovly bride,/but Anna, damn 'er, up and died."*

If you want to try *Anadama bread* use the authentic recipe given in Imogene Wolcott's *The New England Cookbook* (Coward-McCann, 1939). Curse before eating.

"Anchors Aweigh"

> *Anchor's aweigh, my boys, anchor's aweigh.*
> *Farewell to college joys, we sail at break of day!*
> *Through our last night on shore,*
> *Drink to the foam,*
> *Until we meet once more*
> *Here's wishing you a happy voyage home.*

These are the words to "Anchors Aweigh" that were commonly sung by sailors during World War II. But although they are accepted as the lyrics of the song by almost everyone today, they are far different from the original words to the official marching song of the U.S. Navy, which was composed for the 1906 Army-Navy football game, music by Charles A. Zimmerman and lyrics by Alfred H. Miles.

The Andrew

The Andrew has been British slang for the Royal Navy since at least 1860, and *The Andrew Millar* was used long before that. The expression derives from the name of Andrew Millar, or Miller, a notorious press-gang leader of Lord Nelson's day, who shanghaied so many men into the Navy that his victims thought it belonged to him. The term achieved more currency when a firm headed by an Arthur Millar was later awarded a large contract for supplying the Royal Navy with better rations. A common British catch phrase is, "You shouldn't have joined *Andrew* if you couldn't take a joke."

Angle with a Silver Hook

A fisherman who fails to catch anything, doesn't want to go home empty-handed and thus buys fish (with silver coin in past times) to conceal his abject failure is said to *angle with a silver hook*. The phrase dates back to at least the nineteenth century.

Antenna

Antenna was the name the Romans originally applied to a ship's wooden horizontal yarn from which sails were hung. Hundreds of years later, in the sixteenth century, the word was borrowed to describe the "horns" of various insects, such as the snail. In the early twentieth century it was given to the radio and television receptors that we associate *antenna* with today.

Aquanaut, Oceanaut

These words were coined in recent times to describe scientist-explorers who work and live in the sea for long periods. Jacques Cousteau coined *oceanaut* and both words are based on the Greek *nautes*, "sailor."

Archipelago

The *Archipelago* was first the Aegean Sea, the Italians giving the Aegean this name in the thirteenth century from their word *arcipelago*, "chief sea." Later *archipelago* came to mean any sea area containing many scattered islands.

Argonaut

While searching for the Golden Fleece, Jason sailed from Greece to Colchis in the galley *Argo*. His fifty companions were thus called *argonautes*, from the ship's name and the Greek *nautes*, "sailor," and the word *argonaut* is now applied to any adventurer on the sea.

Argosy

Argosy has nothing to do with Jason and the argonauts of Greek legend. The *argosy* was originally a merchant ship built at Ragusa, Dalmatia (now Dubrovnik, Yugoslavia) in the sixteenth century. English sailors called this type of ship a *ragusa* after the port city and this word was corrupted to *ragusy* and then to *argosy*. The name was finally applied to any richly laden merchant vessel.

Armed to the Teeth

Probably some real or imaginary pirate swinging aboard a prize, one hand on a rope, the other hand wielding a cutlass or a pistol, with a knife clamped between his teeth, suggested these words. Anyway, the phrase, still used, if mostly in a humorous way, seems to have originated in the first half of the last century. English politician Richard Cobden used it in 1849, perhaps inspired by an adventure writer of the day.

Around the Horn, Cape Horn

A century ago any sailor who had sailed on a ship around Cape Horn was entitled to spit to windward; otherwise, spitting was a serious infraction of the rules of conduct at sea. Thus, the permissible practice of spitting to windward was called *around the horn*. Cape Horn, incidentally, isn't so named because it is shaped like a horn. Captain

Schouten, the Dutch navigator who rounded it in 1616, named it after Hoorn, his birthplace in northern Holland.

Atlantic Ocean

No one is certain how the Atlantic got its name. It may derive from the fabled kingdom of Atlantis that is said to have existed in its domain, or it could come from the Atlas Mountains in northwest Africa, which the ancients thought overlooked the entire ocean. It is interesting to note that the Atlantic Ocean is widening an inch every year, while the Pacific Ocean is shrinking. This is in accord with the theory of continental drift, which has it that the continents rest upon great plates of the earth's crust and that these plates are constantly moving. North and South America were once joined to Europe and split off, moving away from each other, according to this theory, and as they continue to drift away, the Atlantic grows bigger. The Pacific, however, shrinks as its floor squeezes against Asia. Earth scientists

All hands taking in sail during a storm off Cape Horn
LIBRARY OF CONGRESS

predict that the Atlantic Ocean, which has been growing wider for the past one hundred fifty million years, will continue to grow, while the Pacific Ocean will continue to shrink. In another fifty million years or so, however, many scientists believe that the Atlantic coast of North America will develop into an Andean type of mountain system.

Atlantis, Lemuria, Lyonesse
Plato first mentioned the mythical island of *Atlantis* in the *Timaeus* and *Critias*. Said to have existed in the Atlantic Ocean, Atlantis was supposed to have been destroyed by an earthquake and sunk beneath the bottom of the sea more than ten thousand years ago, which hasn't stopped legions of adventurers from searching for it over the ages. *Lemuria*, said to be near Madagascar, is another famous lost island in history, as is *Lyonnesse*, a mythical country "forty fathoms down" stretching off England from Lands End to the Scilly Isles.

Aunt May
An *Aunt May* is British naval slang for a person generous to sailors. It is aptly named for Mrs. May Hanrahan, the widow of a U.S. naval captain, who "adopted" sixteen British destroyers during World War II and spent almost a quarter of a million dollars on their crews in the form of presents and comforts. *Aunt May* Hanrahan was received by the queen when she visited England after the war and was piped on board the destroyer *Tartar* while a naval band played on the jetty in her honor.

Australia
Captain Matthew Flinders is the second of only two men in history who alone named a continent. The English navigator named *Australia* in 1803 after sailing completely around the continent. It had previously been known from the sixteenth century as *Terra Australis,* "the southern land." For the first man to name a continent see *America* and the story of the map maker who could be credited with naming both North America and South America—though his map only depicted the area we now know as South America and he did not realize that he was naming a continent.

B

Back and Fill

Very little progress is made when you *back and fill* a sailing ship; that is, when you are tacking the craft while the tide is running with her and the wind is against her. In this sailing maneuver, the sails are alternately backed and filled and the ship seems to remain in roughly the same place, going back and then forward. The term was a natural for sailors, and then landlubbers, to apply to any vacillating or irresolute action—to hemming and hawing.

Bailey Bridge

Portable *Bailey bridges*, which were designed to replace bridges destroyed by retreating forces and to carry much heavier loads than military bridges could previously support, were to a large extent responsible for the Allied victory in World War II, particularly in northwestern Europe. They were invented by Sir Donaly Coleman Bailey (b. 1901), an engineer with the British Ministry of Supply, who was knighted in 1945 for his contribution to the war effort. The versatile truss bridges were first used in 1941 and are still employed throughout the world in flood and disaster areas. They are engineering marvels, consisting of some twenty-nine different parts, but made principally of ten-foot-long, five-foot-wide prefabricated lattice-steel panels weighing six hundred pounds that are held together by steel pins.

Bailey bridges, their roadway's timber supported by steel stringers, were often erected in two and three tiers. Amazingly strong, capable of supporting up to one hundred tons on spans 30 feet to 220 feet long, they were of vital help in the rapid advances of Allied troops. A one-hundred-man team could erect a 130-foot span Bailey bridge in one and a half hours in daylight and three hours in total darkness, using very little special equipment. The portable spans were not originally floating pontoon bridges, although they were adapted to this use during the war in the form of *floating Baileys*. Pontoon-type bridges, built over vessels, were employed by the Persians for military purposes as early as 537 B.C. and have been used since time immemorial.

Ballast

Ballast, which helps keep a ship right side up, probably has its ancestor in a Teutonic word meaning "belly load," but no one is sure, though the word has been used for centuries. After unloading her emergency cargo at Corregidor in February 1941, the submarine USS *Trout* took on the most valuable ballast in the history of shipping. No other ballast was available and the *Trout* traveled back to San Francisco loaded with Philippine government gold bars valued at over $9 million.

Balsa Rafts

Sixteenth-century Spanish sailors off South America gave the name *balsa*, meaning "float," to the rafts lashed together with vines that the natives used. They later applied the same name to the tree logs, half the weight of cork, that made the rafts so buoyant. That the rafts make even better boats than the Spaniards suspected was demonstrated by Thor Heyerdahl centuries later when he sailed from South America to Polynesia on a balsa raft, proving that South Americans could have settled Polynesia.

Baltic Sea

The Baltic Sea is named for either the Lithuanian *baltas*, "white," or from the Scandinavian *balta*, "strait." Thus, no one knows for sure whether the Baltic means "the white sea," or "the sea of straits."

Banzai Party

In the days before World War II, when the Japanese Navy and those of the Western powers were on good terms, great *banzai parties*, or shore parties, were held where seamen from Japan and other nations mingled. The expression derives from the general Japanese felicitation *banzai*, which means "May you live forever." During World War II, the once pleasant *banzai* was shouted by Japanese soldiers making bayonet charges.

Barge In
Useful but clumsy flat-bottomed *barges*, probably named from an early Celtic word for *boat,* have been common in England since medieval times. These shallow-water craft are often pulled through canals by conventional vessels or by animals on the bank. But accidents involving the unwieldy vessels were frequent; they were constantly bumping into other boats. By the late nineteenth century, English schoolboys were using the slang term *barge*, "to hustle a person," *to barge about* someone, bump him or move him heavily about. It is this practice, far removed from the water but related to *barges*, that led to the expression *to barge in*—to clumsily or rudely intercede, to butt in—that originated in the early 1900s.

Barnacle
Barnacles take their name from the *barnacle goose*, which is so-called because of it's "bare neck," *barnakylle* in Middle English, for in ancient times people firmly believed that these geese were born from what we now know as *barnacles*. "There are found in northern parts of Scotland," instructed an old scientific description of barnacles, "certain shell fishes of a white colour . . . wherein are contained little living creatures; which shells in time of maturitie do open, and out of them grow these little living fowls whom we call barnacle geese." A quick look at a ship barnacle, which causes damage to ships and piers exceeding $1 billion annually, does show how easily sound observation can lead to the wrong conclusions. A barnacle's long stalk and rounded body clearly resemble the neck and body of a goose, and its tentacles, which wave during the feeding process, suggest the wings of an infant bird being born from a shell and straining out to sea. The ubiquitous crustacean takes its scientific name, *Cirripedes*, from the Greek *cirri*, feetlike curls of hair, in reference to its tentacles.

Batten Down the Hatches

The descriptive building term *batten* means simply a sawed strip of wood. This word gives us the nautical phrase *batten down the hatches*, for battens were used to fasten canvas over a ship's hatchways during a storm.

Bay Window

This window, devised as early as the fourteenth century, is so named because in projecting from the house, it made the room inside appear to mariners like a little harbor or bay.

To Bear Down Upon

The nautical practice of *bearing down* on another ship means to sail toward her rapidly from a position upwind. From this naval strategy comes the phrase *to bear down upon*, to put pressure on someone or something.

Bêche-de-Mer

Bêche-de-mer, a pidgin-English language of the West Pacific, takes its name from the trepang or sea cucumber, which is also called the bêche-de-mer. The bêche-de-mer was much traded in the region as a food item and finally lent its name to the lingua franca that developed between traders of all kinds.

Before the Mast

Seamen on sailing ships in days past always bunked in the forecastle (fo'c'sle), literally before the mast, which accounts for the title of Richard Henry Dana's classic *Two Years Before the Mast* (1840). But *before the mast* also means to be hauled before the mast of a ship, where the captain held court, to be tried for some offense.

Between Scylla and Charybdis

In the *Odyssey*, Homer vividly described Odysseus's passage between Scylla and Charybdis. In Greek mythology Scylla (*Skulla*) was a beautiful maiden loved by Poseidon, the lord of the sea. But her rival, Amphitrite, fed Scylla magic herbs that turned her into a monster with twelve dangling feet, six long necks with a head on each and three rows of teeth. She dwelt in a high cave overlooking the sea (situated, according to tradition, in the Strait of Messina) and from every ship that passed by, each of her terrible mouths reached down and devoured a sailor. On the other side of the narrow channel, beneath an immense wild fig tree, lay a dangerous whirlpool called Charybdis (*Charubdis*) that sucked in and regorged the sea three times a day. It was Odysseus's fate to sail *between Scylla and Charybdis*, as it is still the fate of anyone steering a mid-course between equally dangerous perils. Odysseus had mixed luck: He lost his crew and ship, but saved his own life by clinging to the fig tree at the base of Charybdis.

Between the Devil and the Deep Blue Sea, the Devil to Pay

Satan probably didn't inspire this old saying, as many people believe. It is thought to be a nautical expression, as its earliest recorded use in 1621 indicates, the "devil" in it referring not to Olde Horney but to a seam between planks in a wooden ship's deck, specifically the long seam nearest either side of a ship. This seam was "the devil to get at" and any sailor caulking it in a heavy sea risked falling overboard. The seam that ran around a ship's hull at the waterline, another one difficult and dangerous to get at, was also called the devil, and these two devils inspired the memorable alliterative phrase *between the devil and the deep blue sea*—someone caught on the horns of a dilemma, caught between difficulties equally dangerous.

Similarly, *the devil to pay* refers to *paying*—"waterproofing with pitch"—the devil on a ship. *Pay* here comes from the Latin *picare* for the process, and the original phrase was *the devil to pay and no hot pitch*.

Between Wind and Water

When a ship is struck by a shell or torpedo in an area that is between wind and water—that is, wounded in a part of the hull that dips into the water and then rises to the wind when plowing through rough seas—it is usually seriously damaged. The expression *be-*

tween wind and water has thus been used since the sixteenth century to signify a hazardous wound in a ship and is used metaphorically to mean an unexpected attack on someone.

The Big Drink, Big Ditch, Big Water, Big Pond

The Big Drink, the first humorous American phrase for the Atlantic, Pacific, or any big body of water, seems to have been coined anonymously in 1844 and was also a name for the Mississippi River, which is more commonly called the *Big Ditch* or *Big Water*. *Big Ditch*, coined in 1825, has also been applied to the Atlantic, but is most commonly associated with the Erie Canal. The *Big Pond*, a humorous term for the Atlantic, stems from about 1840, when it was coined by Canadian humorist Thomas Haliburton.

Bilge

Bilge, now meaning nonsense or filth, was originally the dirty water that collected in the bottom of a ship. *Bilge* was first spelled *bulge*, which referred to the fact that the dirty water collected in the bulge or curve at the bottom of a straight-sided ship.

Billingsgate

Billingsgate, coarse and abusive language, is language similar to that used by the fishwives in the Billingsgate fish market along the River Thames in London. The area was named for whoever built the gate below the London Bridge leading to the old walled city. But who built Billing's Gate is a matter of controversy. Some historians credit a Mr. Billings (or Billin, or Belin), a builder or famous burgher who owned property thereabouts; others suggest that Billing's Gate was named for an ancient clan called Billings, or for one Belen (Belinus), a legenday monarch, citing a 1658 map that ascribes it to "Belen, ye 23rd Brittish Kinge." In any case, the real eponym would be glad not to have his name definitively associated with the vile rhetoric of the viragoes who sold fish by his gate.

Biscuits

In order to keep them from quickly spoiling at sea, biscuits were cooked a second time. Thus their name derives from the Latin *bis*, twice, and *coctus*, cooked—"cooked twice."

To the Bitter End

There are two respectable theories regarding the origins of this phrase. The first is that death has always been regarded as *the bitter end*, as in the phrase from *Proverbs*, "Her end is bitter as wormwood." Poetically, then, any unpleasant final result, utter defeat or death would be *the bitter end*. But the anchor rope on early sailing vessels was attached to a device called the *bitt*, from which the anchor and anchor rope were paid out into the sea. The portion of the anchor rope nearest the bitt was called the "bitter end." There was no more anchor rope to be paid out after you came to the *bitter end*, and so you were *at the end of your rope*. This nautical expression became widely known and has undoubtedly helped *to the bitter end* live its long life and may even be the prime source of the phrase.

Blackballing

So infamous was the nineteenth-century Black Ball Steamer line between Liverpool and New York, the pilfering of its sailors widely known on both sides of the Atlantic and second only to the cruelty of its officers, that the term *blackball* came to mean stealing or pilfering at sea—not at all the way a modern shipping line would want to be immortalized in the language.

Blackbirder

Blackbirder was the name for a ship engaged in the African or Polynesian slave trade in the mid-nineteenth century. A *blackbird* was a captive aboard a slaver and *blackbirding* was used to describe such kidnapping or slaving.

Black Maria

Here is one derivation that would be given with a lot of "it is saids" if there was room for them. Maria Lee, an imposing black woman, be-

29

came a national heroine in 1798 when she delivered swivel guns to outfit the little cutters Alexander Hamilton had ordered built to protect American merchant ships on the high seas. One time Maria even demolished a band of smugglers who tried to steal the cannon, making her delivery to the cutter *Scammel* right on time.

Maria was just as reliable when she opened her boardinghouse for sailors in the early 1800s; her place was the cleanest and her guests the best mannered on the Boston waterfront because even hardened criminals feared her awesome strength. In fact, the giant woman once rescued a policeman being attacked. She aided the police so often that the saying "send for the Black Maria" became common whenever there was trouble with an offender. Fiery Maria sometimes helped escort prisoners to jail and when the first British police horse vans or paddy wagons were introduced in 1838, they may have been christened *Black Marias* in her honor. The tradition has skimpy evidence to support it. Critics point out that the first van was *black* and that *Maria* could have come from numerous sources, but no better version has been given and it would be a shame not to mention a good story.

Black Sea

Never give a derogatory name to any natural force, good or bad, the ancient Greeks believed. So they named what we know as the *Black Sea*, the Euxine or "the Hospitable," even though it was noted for its storms and rocky shores. Later, the Turks named it the Black Sea because they were terrified of its dangers and large stretches of open water.

Black-Shoe Navy

A derogatory term for the seafaring navy coined by members of its air arm. Navy fliers, usually not Annapolis graduates, were allowed to wear brown shoes, while the dress code specified black shoes for all others. The airborne officers felt that promotions came too easily for the Annapolis men and *Black-shoe navy* was the kindest of the epithets they hurled at them.

Blazer

Some authorities believe that the jacket called the *blazer* takes its name from the "somewhat striking blue-and-white-striped jerseys" that the captain of Britain's H.M.S. *Blazer* ordered his crew to wear in the nineteenth century. Others, more cautious and probably right, say the jackets were called blazers because they were the "brightest possible blazing scarlet." The jackets, according to this theory, were first worn by the crew of the *Lady Margaret*, St. John's College, Cambridge, Boat Club in 1889.

Blighia sapida, *Captain Bligh*

A *Captain Bligh*, commemorating the captain of *Mutiny on the Bounty* fame, is still used to describe a cruel, coldhearted task-master. Captain William Bligh is also remembered by the akee fruit, which looks and tastes like scrambled eggs when properly prepared, but can be poisonous when over- or underripe. The akee tree's botanical name is *Blighia sapida,* after the man who introduced it along with breadfruit. Bligh was called "Breadfruit Bligh" for his discovery of that fruit's virtues and was in fact bringing specimens of the breadfruit tree from Tahiti to the West Indies in 1789 when his mutinous crew foiled his plans. The lesson of the *Bounty* apparently taught him little or nothing, for his harsh methods and terrible temper aroused a second mutiny, the Rum Rebellion, while he served as governor of New South Wales. Bligh, a brave and able officer, retired from the navy a vice admiral. He died in 1817 at the age of sixty-three.

Blue Lights

Blue lights became a term for traitors during the War of 1812 when on December 12, 1813, pro-British Americans flashed blue lights to British ships off the coast as a signal that Commodore Stephen Decatur's two frigates would soon be sailing from their New London, Connecticut, harbor. Acting on this information, the British blockaded the port. *Blue lights*, almost obsolete today, would continue to be a synonym for *traitor* until the 1850s.

Blue-Nose Certificate

"We Neptunus, Monarch of all Seas, do hereby declare that Our Loyal Subject _____ on this day hath passed north of the Arctic Circle into the Realms of the Midnight Sun. Having thus penetrated the rigours of the frozen north, it is Our Royal Privilege to bestow upon him the Ancient and Universally Honoured Diploma of the Blue Nose. Given under Sovereign Hand on this day _____ on board the Ship _____."

Such was the *blue-nose certificate,* an illuminated diploma once awarded aboard British vessels to those who had crossed a meridian north of the Arctic Circle, the "blue-nose" referring, of course, to the cold. So far as is known, the certificate is no longer awarded.

Blue Peter

When a ship is ready to leave port, a signal flag called the *blue peter* is raised to call all crew members aboard and to notify everyone in port that all money claims must be settled because the ship is departing. The flag is blue with a white square in the center. Why the peter in the term? Some authorities believe it is a corruption of the French *partir*, "to depart," while most consider it to be a telescoping of the word *repeater.* According to the majority theory, the naval flag was originally used as a "repeater flag," a signal flag hoisted to indicate that a signal from another ship hadn't been read and should be repeated.

Blue-Water Sailor

Blue-water sailor is a complimentary title for a sailor who customarily sails in the "deep [blue] sea" as opposed to coastal waters.

Boatswain, Bos'n

Bos'n is a corruption of *boatswain,* the boy or *swain* who took care of the ship's boat and summoned its crew. The *boatswain* didn't get his whistle until sometime in the fifteenth century and wasn't called a *bos'n* for two hundred years more.

Bonanza

Our word for a rich body of gold or silver ore in a mine, or any rich strike, began life as a Spanish word meaning "fair weather at sea." Miners in California probably learned the word from seamen, who also used it to mean prosperity in general, and applied *bonanza* to any rich body of ore.

Bonaparte's Gull

Bonaparte's gull, one of only two black-headed species in the United States, was described scientifically for the first time in Prince Charles Lucien Bonaparte's *American Ornithology, or History of Birds Inhabiting the United States not Given by Wilson.* Bonaparte, Napoleon's nephew, resided in this country from 1824 to 1833. The gull bearing the naturalist's name breeds hundreds of miles from the sea, becoming a seabird in winter. Inland bird watchers consider it a harbinger of spring.

Booby Hatch

Sailors on old vessels were sometimes punished by being confined in the *booby hatch*, a hatch covered with a wooden hood that led to the forepeak of the vessel. This booby hatch, with screaming sailors in it, may have given us the expression *booby hatch* for an insane asylum, though there is no strong proof for the theory.

Boot, Boot Camp

During the Spanish-American War, sailors wore leggings called *boots*, which came to mean a navy (or marine) recruit. These recruits trained in *boot camps*.

Bosum Bread

These were large, flat loaves of bread that black stevedores working the Mississippi steamboats carried in their shirt fronts (against their chests or *bosums*) for snacks throughout the day. Such energy they needed, as these longshoremen expended more energy than almost any other workers in the nineteenth century. Even today barge workers in the Netherlands consume more calories than any other occupational group, consuming an average of 5300 calories a workday.

Botany Bay

Captain James Cook named Botany Bay after the many new botanical specimens he found there on his voyage to Australia in 1770. Later, the inlet's name came to be wrongly applied to a convict settlement at Sydney, even to the whole of Australia.

Boys of the Bulldog Breed

Boys of the bulldog breed are pugnacious Englishmen, often sailors. These words come from the popular nineteenth-century song "Sons of the Sea, All British Born."

Bread Crumbs; Fork in the Beam

Naval discipline was much harder to take a century or so ago. For example, when a senior officer cried, *"Bread crumbs!"* in the British Navy at that time, it was a signal that junior midshipmen in their mess were not to hear what was going to be said next and actually had to stuff their ears with bread until the senior officers finished speaking. Similarly, when a senior officer placed a *fork in the deck beam* above his head, it meant that he wanted privacy and all junior midshipmen had to leave the mess.

Bride of the Sea

In the early eleventh century, the wedding of the Doge of Venice to the Adriatic symbolized the sea power of Venice. Every year the Doge, in his state barge, the *Bucentaur*, sailed into the Adriatic on Ascension Day and dropped a wedding ring into the sea. This practice, still part of the annual ceremony called the *Sposalizo del Mar*, is responsible for Venice's historical name "The Bride of the Sea."

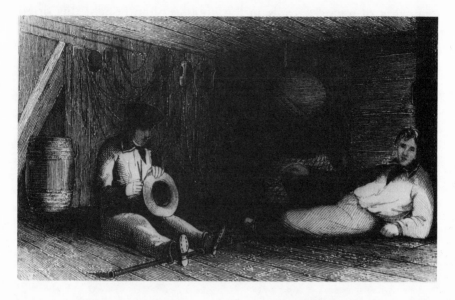

Sailors shackled in the brig on a nineteenth-century vessel.

Brig

This word for a prison cell on board ship must still be marked "origin unknown," but there are some interesting theories about its derivation. The term is an Americanism first recorded in 1852. One theory has it that pirates called *brigands* sailed on *brigandines* or *brigantines*, small two-masted sailing vessels, their name soon shortened to *brig*. Since the *brigands* were criminals often in jail, the name of the type of ship they sailed was associated with jail cells.

Buccaneer, Freebooter, Corsair

Buccaneer was the name applied to themselves by the sea raiders roaming the Caribbean, who claimed they were privateers, although this wasn't always the case, and they often attacked any ship in time of peace or war. The word *buccaneer* itself derives from the *boucanes*, or little dome-shaped smokehouses, on Hispaniola Island, where strips of boar and cattle meat were smoked dry over a slow fire. The men who smoked *viando boucanee* or "jerky" and sold it in bundles of a hundred for six pieces of eight were called *boucaniers*, "smokers of meat." Pirates in the area so often bought this dried meat from the *boucaniers*—it was a perfect food to carry in the days before processed meat—that they began to be called *boucaniers* or *buccaneers*, too.

Freebooter was another term for *buccaneer*, as was *filibuster*, which is simply English for the mispronounced French word for freebooter—*flibustier*—*freebooter* being difficult for the French to pronounce!

Corsair was a Spanish word for someone between a pirate and a privateer, while *sea robbers* and *sea rovers* were German and Dutch inventions also carelessly applied. At any rate, very few of these thieves of the sea were not under the skin the *hostes humani generi*, "enemies of the human race," that the Roman orator Cicero called all pirates centuries ago—though it is important to note that almost all pirates euphemistically called themselves "privateers," or "brethren of the coast." (See also *Pirates*.)

Bumboat

Bumboats (also called *dirtboats*) were first, in the early seventeenth century, scavengers' boats used to remove filth from ships anchored in the Thames. Their name ultimately derives from the medieval *bum* for the buttocks, a word of echoic origin imitative of "the sound of breaking wind." The *bumboats'* crews used to sell fresh vegetables to the ships in the harbor, so these craft came to be known as "any boat employed to carry provisions, vegetables and small merchandise for sale to ships, either in port or lying at a distance from shore."

Buoy, Buoyant

Though it is pronounced *boy* in England and by many sailors and some landlubbers in America (as in Lifebuoy soap), the word *buoy* (often pronounced *boo-i*) has no etymological connection with *boy*. *Buoy* comes from the Old French *boye* meaning "chained," in reference to the chain that holds a buoy in place. However, the chain is invisible to anyone looking at a buoy and buoys came, ironically enough, to suggest lightness and freedom (the opposite of being chained) to onlookers, giving us the words *buoyant* and *buoyancy*.

Burn Your Bridges Behind You

It is said that the expression was originally *burn your boats behind you*, which originated with the Romans. Roman generals, including Caesar, often did burn all their boats after invading an alien land to impress upon their legions the fact that there could be no retreat: The only way they'd get back to Rome would be through a victorious campaign. Later, bridges were burned for the same reason and the phrase to *burn your bridges behind you* came to mean, figuratively, to take a stand from which no honorable withdrawal is possible.

By and Large

The nautical term *by and large* originated in the days of sailing ships and roughly means to sail a ship to the wind and off it. These instructions to a helmsman were not precise and so the seventeenth-century nautical term came to indicate imprecise generalities in everyday English and to mean "generally speaking," "on the whole" —especially when the speaker or writer is telling the substantial truth, despite minor exceptions. Literal-minded linguists and sailors object to the use of the expression because *by and large* really describes a more complex marine operation than is indicated in the above definition, but trying to mop it out of English now would be a *Partingtonian task*. (See *Dame Partington*.)

Cannibal, Caliban, Caribbean Sea

When Columbus encountered the Caribs upon landing in the Lesser Antilles on his second voyage in 1943, these natives gave him their name as *Canibales*. This word was merely a dialectic form of *Caribes* and these people were Caribs themselves, but the Spanish thereafter called the whole Carib tribe *Canibales*. Because some of these fierce, bold warriors ate human flesh, within a century their name was used in Europe as a synonym for *man-eaters*, and *cannibalism* was substituted for the classical *anthropophagy*. The word was probably also influenced by the Spanish word *canino*, meaning "canine" or "voracious." Columbus, incidentally, thought he had landed in Asia and that the *Canibales* were subjects of the Great Khan, or Cham, another doubtful but possible influence on the word's formation.

The Caribs of the South American coast were far more adventurous and warlike than those of the larger islands like Cuba, and it is from these expert mariners—they were one of the few New World peoples to use sails—that the *Caribbean Sea* takes its name. In fact, at the time of Columbus, the natives in the Lesser Antilles spoke two separate languages, the men one and the women another. This situation developed when fierce South American Caribs invaded the islands some years before, butchering and eating all the relatively peaceful Arawak male inhabitants and claiming their women. In retaliation, the women devised a separate "female language" based on Arawak, refusing to speak *Carib* and maintaining silence in the presence of all males, a revenge that they practiced for generations afterward.

Another word derived from the Caribs or Canibales is Shakespeare's Caliban—Prospero's half-human slave in *The Tempest*, and hence any bestial, degraded man. *Caliban* was probably formed by either metathesis from the Spanish *canibal* or as a variant of *Cariban*, a Carib.

Canopy

The *canopy* held over kings and the *canopy* we know as an overhanging protection or shelter both take their name from *konops*, the Greek for *gnat.* The first canopy was a "gnat curtain" that fishermen and boatmen on the Nile River fashioned from their fine-meshed nets and slept under to protect themselves from gnats.

Cape Cod Turkey

Baked codfish has been called *Cape Cod turkey* in New England and elsewhere for many years, at least since the mid-nineteenth century, just as melted cheese has been called *Welsh rabbit* the world over.

Cape of Good Hope

Portuguese explorer Bartholomeu Dias named this treacherous area off the southern tip of Africa "Cape of Storms." However, King John II of Portugal changed the name to *Cape of Good Hope* to encourage exploration of the area! Earlier the Vikings had played the same public relations game when naming Greenland, which was hardly green.

A Captain Cook

On one of the great explorer's historic voyages, Captain James Cook and his men introduced the domesticated pig to New Zealand. Many of these animals escaped into the wild and multiplied; there were so many that settlers took to calling the wild pigs *captain cooks*, a name they retain to this day.

Captain of the Heads

A jocular Navy term for the enlisted man responsible for keeping the lavatories or *heads* neat and clean. Wrote one proud mother to a friend: "My son is doing very well in the Navy. In only six months he's been promoted to Captain of the Heads!" *Heads* are so called because they were originally in the bow or head of a ship.

Captain Outrageous and Company: Piratical Pseudonyms

Blackbeard, Diabolito, Long Knife, Captain Buzzard, Gentleman Harry, Big John, Black Bart, and Calico Jack—these are only a few of the many pirates who chose to live under colorful pseudonyms that they invented or had bestowed upon them. The pirate with the oldest *nom de guerre*, however, must be the French pirate Captain Borgne-Fosse, whose pseudonym translates as Captain Half-Ass, an appellation about which history remains silent.

Careen

To *careen* a ship is to ground her at high tide, and when the tide has receded to heel her over on her side. It is sometimes done with small vessels so their bottoms can be scraped, caulked or otherwise repaired. The word is first recorded in the late sixteenth century and derives from the French *carène*, "keel," which comes from the Latin *carina*, "keel." A ship is also said to *careen* when she inclines to one side or lies over when sailing on a wind. From this nautical expression comes our term for any leaning, swaying or tipping to one side of something while it is in motion, such as, "The car careened around the corner."

Catamaran

This twin-hulled sailboat has nothing to do with mountain lions or catamounts, even though it can get wild when the wind is blowing hard. *Catamaran* has its origins in a Tamil word that means "logs tied together," and the craft originated in the Indian Ocean area.

Catch a Crab

Oarsmen who *catch a crab* of course don't literally catch one on an oar. The expression means that the oarsman has slowed down the speed of the boat by either missing the water on a stroke, or, more commonly, by making a poor, awkward stroke that doesn't completely clear the water when completed.

Cat-o'-nine-tails

The British Navy only stopped using the *cat-o'-nine-tails* as an instrument of punishment in 1881, but it can still be used legally in England as a punishment for certain violent crimes, though it rarely is. Some black humorist probably coined the name for this terrible scourge—because it "scratched" the back like a cat—but the fact that the first Egyptian scourges were made of thongs of cat hide may have had something to do with the word's origin. The nine tails of the scourge, similar to the "nine lives of a cat," could also have suggested the name. Scourging criminal offenders with a whip is a punishment as old as history. There are cases in medieval England of prisoners receiving sixty thousand stripes from whips with three lashes and twenty knots in each tail. But the *cat-o'-nine-tails*, com-

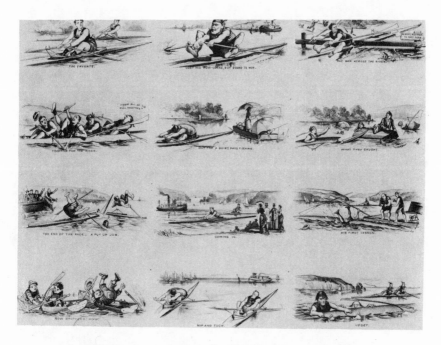

An early (1878) precursor of the comic strip poked fun at rowers, many of whom would frequently catch a crab.

LIBRARY OF CONGRESS

posed of one eighteen-inch handle with nine tails and three or more knots on each tail, only dates back to about 1670. Men were flayed alive with this scourge, which people believed was more holy, and thus effective, because its nine tails were a "trinity of trinities" ($3 \times 3 = 9$).

Cat's-paw

Light air during a calm that moves as silently as a cat and causes ripples on the water, indicating a coming storm to sailors, is called a *cat's-paw*. The term is recorded as early as 1769. Captain Frederick Marryat wrote in *Jacob Faithful* (1834): "Cat's paws of wind, as they call them, flew across the water here and there, ruffling its smooth surface." *Cat's-paw* can also mean a certain nautical knot.

A cat-o'-nine-tails used to flog a seaman on a nine-teenth-century man-of-war

A sturgeon, from which the most expensive caviar comes

MEYERS ANIMAL LEXICON, *1895*

Cat the Anchor
Catting the anchor simply means to keep the anchor clear of the ship by hanging it outside the vessel on a piece of timber called the *cathead.*

Caviar
"I heard thee speak me a speech once," Hamlet says to the players at Elsinore, "but it was never acted . . . ; for the play, I remember, pleased not the million, 'twas caviar to the general." When Shakespeare says "general" here, he means the general public, the generality, the masses as they were later called, not the general of an army. The play he refers to (which was actually pretty bad judging by the fragments presented) is, like caviar, for the tastes of only the most discriminating people; others would find it repugnant because

43

they haven't acquired fine tastes. The rather snobbish remark is still commonplace in describing something for which one has to acquire a taste.

Caviar derives from the Turkish *havyar,* salted sturgeon eggs. The Russians call the fish eggs *ikra*, not caviar, and it is from a select sturgeon species called the Beluga that the highly regarded *Beluga caviar* comes. Actually, the most prized caviar of all is that made from selected golden sterlet's eggs of the *Acipenser ruthenus* species, produced by sterlets "with a particularly happy frame of mine." While dispelling myths about caviar, we should mention that *malossol* isn't a quality name like *Beluga*; it is just less salty caviar and you can buy *Beluga malossol, Sevruga malossol,* et cetera. Caviar lovers have always been more general than Shakespeare knew. In America caviar was once so plentiful that we shipped it to Europe; it was so cheap here that caviar sandwiches were free in saloons with a nickel glass of beer.

A Cecil's Fast
Hoping to improve the fish trade in England, Queen Elizabeth's long-time minister William Cecil, Lord Burghley, had legislation passed requiring Englishmen to eat fish and no meat on certain days of the week. Beef-eating and mutton-eating Britons didn't like the idea much and dubbed all fish dinners *Cecil's fasts.* Possibly the idea remained distasteful to Englishmen for over two centuries, because in the early 1800s cold hash patties were being called *Cecils*—another substitute for "real" meat.

Charley More
"Charley More—the fair (or square) thing" was the legend on the huge tavern sign of a Maltese publican about 1840. His name became synonymous with fair or straight dealing and *Charley More* has long been a British naval term for one who is honest and upright.

Charley Noble
Another British Navy term dating from the nineteenth century. Commander, captain, or ship's cook Charles Noble (c. 1840) demanded that the cowl of the copper funnel of his galley stove always be kept

brightly polished. Up until about 1900, galley funnels were called *Charley Nobles* in his honor. Or so the old story goes.

Cheapskate

During the Revolutionary War, American soldiers liked to sing the Scottish song "Maggie Lauder," the chorus of which chided a *blatherskite*, a gabby person full of nonsense or hot air. The song is a very old one dating back to the seventeenth century and the word *blatherskite* is older still: It is formed from *bladder*, an obsolete English word for an inflated, pretentious man, a windbag, and a contemptuous use of the word *skate*, referring to the common food fish. Why the *skate* was chosen for the humorous word isn't clear—perhaps because a skate was believed to inflate itself like a blowfish, or possibly just because it was a common fish. In any case, "Maggie Lauder" made *blatherskite* popular here in America and later in the nineteenth century, when we invented our native word *cheapskate* for a tightwad, we borrowed the *skate* from it. This is a more roundabout explanation than the theory that the *skate* in *cheapskate* comes from a British slang word for "chap," but it seems more logical as *skate* in the form of "chap" never had any real currency here.

Chew the Fat (Rag)

Chewing the fat can mean grousing or just talking idly. When first recorded as military slang in Brunlees Paterson's *Life in the Ranks* (1885), it meant the former. One guess is that the expression was originally a nautical one: Sailors working their jaws on the tough salt pork rationed out when supplies ran low constantly grumbled about their poor fare while chewing the fat. *Chewing the rag* also had a grouchy connotation when first recorded in print at about the same time. There are a few stories relating these words to *real* rag chewing (men chewing pieces of rags when out of tobacco and grousing about it, et cetera), but more than likely the expression has its roots in the English verb *to rag*, "to scold," its origin unknown. Both phrases are probably much older than their first appearance in print and both are used more often today for a talkfest between friends than for grumbling about something.

Chow

Chowchow was originally a European approximation of the Chinese word for mixed pickles, but has come to mean any mixed dish. British sailors who were fed a lot of mixed dishes in the nineteenth century shortened the word to *chow* and applied it to meals or food in general.

Chubby

Since the early seventeenth century short, fat people have been called *chubby* after the thick, fat and round-cheeked fish named the *chub,* a type of carp common in England and northern Europe. American fish called *chub* are not the same fish at all.

Chunnel

Chunnel is the name for the tunnel under the English Channel from England to France, which has long been discussed but has not been constructed, mainly because of English fears of invasion from Europe through it.

CINCUS, FIB

No doubt the most embarrassing naval acronym in history was CIN-CUS (pronounced "sink us"), which stood for the *C*ommander *in* *C*hief of the *U*nited *S*tates Navy before World War II, but was dropped from use in the reorganization of the Navy following Pearl Harbor. Another amusing nautical acronym is FIB, standing for the *F*isherman's *I*nformation *B*ureau of Chicago. The *Guinness Book of World Records* claims that the longest English acronym is the twenty-two-letter ADCOMSUBORDCOMPHIBSPAC, used in the U.S. Navy to denote the Administrative Command: Amphibious Forces, Pacific Fleet, Subordinate Command. But there is at least one longer one: the twenty-six-letter COMSUBCOMNEIMCOMHEDSUPPACT, which stands for Command, Subordinate Command, U.S. Naval Forces Eastern Atlantic and Mediterranean, Commander Headquarters Support Activities—itself abbreviated as CSCN/CHSA.

Cinque Ports
Special privileges were granted by the Crown from the thirteenth to the seventeenth centuries and even later to the ports of Hastings, Sandwich, Dover, Romaney and Hythe, because they provided men and ships for the defense of the English Channel. Later the ports of Rye and Winchelsea were added, but the ports were still called *cinque* ports from the Latin *quinque*, five.

A Clean Bill of Health
This widely used term has its origins in the document issued to a ship showing that the port it sails from suffered from no epidemic or infection at the time of departure. Less widely used is the term *a foul bill of health*, meaning the opposite.

Cleopatra's Pearl
Cleopatra and Mark Antony always did things for each other. Legend has it that she once filled a room ankle-high with rose petals so that he would not hear his footsteps when he walked. And Mark Antony was so pleased with a dinner a chef prepared for Cleopatra that he made the cook a gift of a city all his own. *Cleopatra's pearl* concerns a sumptuous banquet Cleopatra gave for Antony. Her lover, the story tells us, expressed astonishment at the costly meal, and she promptly removed a pearl earring, dropped it in a cup of vinegar and let it dissolve, saying, "My draft [the cost of this banquet] to Antony shall far exceed it." Vinegar cannot dissolve a pearl, however, and anything strong enough to do so wouldn't have conveniently been on Cleopatra's table. Unless the wileful woman planted it there—in which case it is just as possible that she used a fake pearl. Sir Thomas Gresham is said to have repeated this episode with Queen Elizabeth, grinding a precious £15,000 gem to dust, mixing it in his glass of wine and drinking to the Virgin Queen's health.

Clipper Ship
While the origin of the *clipper* in *clipper ship* is not definitely known, it may be yet another word that we owe to Cleopatra. The first authentic *clipper ship* was the *Ann McKim,* built in Baltimore in 1832, but an early French ship of this type was christened *Cleopatra-cum-*

Antonio. The French ship's name, some scholars say, was shortened in usage to *Clipster* and then to *Clipper*, the last becoming the designation for all vessels of this class. Other authorities contend that rude *clippers* were being built before the War of 1812 and were known as *Baltimore clippers* because they literally clipped the surface of the sea. Still another source holds that the expression "going at a clip" resulted in the word; and some investigators even claim that *clipper* is an invention of either Robert Burns or Percy Bysshe Shelley. But the French developed the principle for this type of ship in the eighteenth century, long before the *Baltimore clippers*, and as the *Cleopatra-cum-Antonio* dates from that period, the Cleopatra theory has much to say for it. The long, narrow *clipper ship*, with its "cloud of sails" and carrying commerce to the far corners of the world, revolutionized sea travel, sailing at up to 18 knots as it cleaved the waves. Some famous *clippers* were the *Cutty Sark*—which once covered 363 miles in a day's travel—the *Flying Cloud*, the *Sea Witch*, the *Witch of the Waves*, and the *Nightingale.* The age of this last and fastest of the great sailing vessels ended when the prosaic steamship began to forge past it. *Clipper ship* was later applied to transoceanic flying boats, the famed *Flying Clippers.*

The Coast Is Clear
Prominent during Prohibition among liquor smugglers, *the coast is clear* is a much older term that passed into general use in the nineteenth century. It originally meant that no coast guards were in sight and it was safe to sail in certain waters.

Coconut
Safe in its buoyant, waterproof pod, the *coconut* drifted in the high seas from southern Asia in prehistoric times and was propagated and cultivated throughout tropical regions. But it wasn't given its name until the late fifteenth century, when Portuguese sailors came upon it in the Indian Ocean islands and fancied that the little indentations at the base of the nut looked like eyes. Thinking that these three "eyes" gave the nut the look of a grinning face, they named it the *coconut, côco* being the Portuguese word for "a grinning face." The nut deserves a better appellation, having been "the fruit of life" for ages, providing people with food, drink, oil, medicines, fuel and

even bowls, not to mention the many uses of the sixty- to -one-hundred-foot tree on which it grows. *Copra*, important to the plot of many a South Sea tale, is the dried meat of coconuts that oil is pressed from, and *coconut* itself is slang for a head, which takes the word back to its origins.

Coconut Crab

Although the large *robber* or *coconut crab* (*Birgus latro*) of the Pacific islands is closely related to the hermit crab, it has given up carrying a portable dwelling and developed a permanent hard-plated shell. Named the coconut crab because it climbs palm trees to get the fruit, it is called the *robber crab* for an entirely different reason. After chasing another land crab, *Cardisoma*, into its hole in the ground, the robber crab threatens to enter. When *Cardisoma* thrusts out its big claw to guard the entrance, the robber crab seizes it, twists it off, and scuttles away to enjoy a gourmet feast.

The coast isn't clear for smugglers when any of these Coast Guard cutters are in the vicinity.

U.S. COAST GUARD

49

Cod, Sacred Cod, You Can't Cod Me

Experts have suggested that *cod* might derive from an old Danish word for "bag" (because it was thought to be a "bag fish," in reference to its shape), but its origin must be marked unknown due to lack of evidence, even though the word has been with us at least since the fourteenth century. The North Atlantic cod (*Gadus morrhua*), reaching a length of up to three feet and a weight of up to fifty pounds, has long been one of the most important fish of commerce (see *Codfish Aristocracy*). It is called the *sacred cod* because it is said to be the fish that Christ multiplied and fed to the multitude. According to one early nineteenth-century writer: "Even today the marks of His thumbs and forefingers are plainly visible on the codfish. His Satanic majesty stood by and said he, too, could multiply fish and feed multitudes. Reaching for one of the fish it wriggled and slid down his red-hot fingers, burning two black stripes down its side and thus clearly differentiating the haddock from the sacred cod. These markings, in actual practice, do distinguish one fish from another." *You can't cod me* means "You can't get a rise out of me, you won't make me rise to the bait like a codfish."

Codfish Aristocracy

> *Of all the fish that swim or swish*
> *In oceans deep autocracy,*
> *There's none possesses such haughtiness*
> *As the codfish aristocracy.*
>
> —WALLACE IRWIN

It's hard to think of any group haughtier than the Cabots and Lowells (who spoke only to God, according to another old poem), but the Boston nouveau riche who made their money from the codfishing industry in the late eighteenth and early nineteenth century apparently gave a grand imitation of them. At any rate, they were disliked enough to inspire the derogatory expression *codfish aristocracy* for any pretentious, newly rich person.

Columbus's Egg

Washington Irving told this proverbial tale in his *History of . . . Christopher Columbus.* It relates a classic squelch supposedly made by Columbus at a banquet given by Cardinal Mendoza shortly after the explorer had returned from his first voyage:

> A shallow courtier present, impatient of the honors paid to Co-
> lumbus, abruptly asked him whether he thought that in case he
> had not discovered the Indies, there were not other men in
> Spain who would have been capable of the enterprise. To this
> Columbus made no immediate reply, but taking an egg, invited
> the company to make it stand on end. Every one attempted it,
> but in vain. Whereupon he struck it upon the table so as to
> break the end and left it standing on the broken part; illustrat-
> ing in his simple manner that when he had once shown the way
> to the New World nothing was easier than to follow it.

Although Irving had the tale on good authority, it may really apply to an earlier historical figure, an Italian architect named Filippo
Brunelleschi.

Come Hell or High Water

The ancestor of this common expression is apparently *between the devil and the deep blue sea* (see page 27). *Between hell and high water* seems to have been a twentieth-century variation on (or de-
viation from) the *devil* phrase. Then the *hell and high water* part took on a life of its own in the expression *come hell or high water*, meaning "no matter what," as in "Come hell or high water, I'll finish it!"

Constellation

Though there is some question about her authenticity (some histo-
rians say she was broken up in 1854 and an entirely new ship built in her place), the *Constellation*, launched in 1797, is still called the oldest American warship afloat and honored as a national shrine in her slip in Baltimore harbor. She was, of course, renowned in her time for her valiant battle against the French *Insurgente* in 1799. "We

would put any man to death on this ship for looking pale," said an officer of her crew.

The Continental Navy

America had a *Colonial Navy* until 1631, but this was replaced by the fifty-three-ship *Continental Navy* in 1776 after the break with Great Britain. Commodore Esek Hopkins was appointed its commander in

So popular was the Constellation *in her day that several songs were written in her honor.*

LIBRARY OF CONGRESS

chief (the only time a Navy head has held that title aside from Presidents). The *Continental Navy* became the *United States Navy* in 1794.

To Coot

Applied to tortoises the obsolete verb *coot* meant "to copulate." Recorded in 1667, its origin is unknown, but it is responsible for the name of two amorous American turtles commonly called the *cooter*—the Carolina box turtle (*Cistudo carolina*) and the Florida cooter (*Chrysemys concinna*). The first recorded use of the word: "The Tortoises . . . coot for fourteen daies together."

Copenhagen

In 1807 the British destroyed the Danish fleet in a surprise attack off Copenhagen. As a result, all surprise attacks came to be called *Copenhagens* after the site of the original battle.

Coral

Coral, deriving from an old Greek word, first meant the beautiful red coral of the Red Sea and the Mediterranean; then it was extended to mean coral of all colors. In ancient times red coral was a highly prized precious gem and was believed to be a charm against shipwreck, lightning, whirlwinds and fire aboard ship. The Romans hung it in necklaces around the necks of infants to "preserve and fasten their teeth." Children were also given coral toys to cut their teeth on. The Norse believed that coral was fashioned beneath the waves by the god Marmendill.

Corvette

Corvettes have become swift armored cruisers, but they were originally cumbersome, ponderous freighters, "old baskets" that took their name from the Latin *corbis*, "basket."

Coxswain

A *coxswain* or *cockswain* was at first the *swain* (boy servant) in charge of the small *cock* or *cockboat* that was kept aboard for the

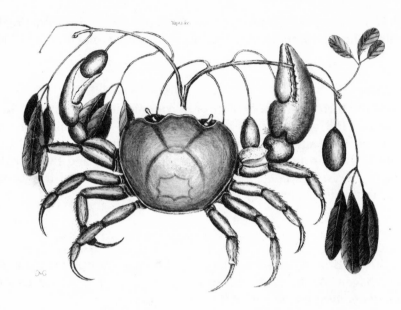

ship's captain and which was used to row him to and from the ship. With the passing of time the *coxswain* became the helmsman of any boat, regardless of size.

Crabby

According to Jacob Grimm, the German word *Krabbe*, from which our *crabby* ultimately derives, meaning a cross, ill-tempered person, owes its origin to the crab, "because these animals are malicious and do not easily let go of what they have." Another authority has it that the primary reference here is "to the crooked or wayward gait of the crustacean, and the contradictory, perverse and fractious disposition which this expresses." Said one early astrologist: "He who is born under Cancer shall be crabbed and angry, because the crab fish is so inclined."

Crazy as a Coot, Crazy as a Loon

As far back as the eighteenth century the coot's stupid facial expressions and clownish behavior inspired the expressions *silly as a coot, stupid as a coot,* and *crazy as a coot.* "During the breeding season

Fulica americana acts especially odd, breaking water, flapping wings, sitting on their tails, slashing at one another with taloned feet and thrusting with their bills," one expert explains. Similarly, the common loon (*Gavia immer*) is noted for what another expert calls its "mirthless laughter," a "high, far-carrying, liquid tremolo that sets your spine atingle." This water bird's name may come from the Dutch *loen, Homo stupidis*, being applied first to stupid people, then to the bird. The loon has nothing to do with the word *loony, crazy*, which is a shortening of *lunatic*.

Crocodile Tears, Alligator

Possessing no tear glands, crocodiles can't shed real tears, though their eyes are kept moist by various secretions. Nevertheless, the myth arose in early times that the crocodile moaned and cried to attract the sympathetic and helpful and then snatched and ate their saviors "wepynge" ("weeping"), as British adventurer and nature faker Sir John Maundeville, the first to record the legend, put it in about 1400. The story was repeated in *Hakluyt's Voyages* (1600) and by many other writers, including Shakespeare, these hypocritical *crocodile's tears* becoming a term for any feigned or hypocritical sorrow. The crocodile takes its name from the Greek *kroke*, "gravel," and *drilos*, "worm," the newly hatched animal resembling to early observers an oversized worm emerging from gravel on the banks of the Nile. Many myths exist about the giant lizard, which probably ranks second only to poisonous snakes as a killer of humans. The *alligator*, less dangerous but hardly a desirable swimming companion, is also a giant lizard and takes its name from the Spanish *legarto*, "lizard." *El lagarto*, as the Spanish called the great Florida reptile, sounded like *alligater* to American ears and this finally became our *alligator*.

Crossing the Line

Crossing the line is sailing across the international date line, an occasion that in days past was celebrated with an initiation ceremony for those who were crossing for the first time. The custom, still practiced to a limited extent, called for a sailor, dressed as King Neptune, and his court to seize novices and lather and shave them, among other horseplay. Today, certificates are often given to those *crossing the line* for the first time.

Crow's Nest

Every ship's highest lookout station is called the *crow's nest* because old sailing vessels once carried a coop high up on their masts in which land birds, including crows, were kept. If winds carried a ship out of sight of land, the birds would be released and the ship would be steered to follow them inland.

Cut Neither Nails nor Hair at Sea

This old superstition, which goes back at least to the ancient Romans, has it that the cuttings of nails and hair were votive offerings to Persephone, Queen of Hades. Therefore, Neptune, ruler of the sea, would be jealous and show his displeasure if sailors cut their nails or hair because he would believe his subjects were making offerings to another god and wreck their ship or drown them.

The Cut of His Jib

Since the cut of a jib or foresail of a ship indicates her character to a sailor and *jib* means "face" in sailor's slang, *I don't like the cut of his jib* translates as "I'm suspicious of him; I don't like the expression on his face."

To Cut the Painter

The *painter* is the rope by which a ship's boat can be tied to the ship, a buoy, or a dock, and the word ultimately derives from the Latin *pendere*, "to hang." Thus *to cut the painter*, a phrase much used in the nineteenth century, came to mean "to sever all connection" with anything.

Dallia Blackfish

This tasty fish honors scientist William Healey Dall (1845–1927), an authority on marine life for the Smithsonian Institution. A pupil of the great Louis Agassiz at Harvard, Dall later wrote one of the first books on Alaska's immense resources. The edible blackfish of Alaska called the *Dallia*, a species of the genus *Dalliidae*, does honor to his pioneer work in the territory.

Dame Partington, Mrs. Partington

English politician and author Sydney Smith alluded to the legendary Dame Partington in an 1831 speech condemning the opposition of the House of Lords to reform measures. Dame Partington had tried to mop up the Atlantic Ocean, which was flooding her cottage in Devon. Thanks mainly to Smith, her name became synonymous for anyone futilely trying to hold back progress or natural forces. The good lady is also remembered as another Mrs. Malaprop, for American humorist Benjamin Shillaber later depicted her, in a number of books and stories, especially the *Life and Sayings of Mrs. Partington* (1854), as a gossipy Yankee woman who constantly misused words. Critics charged Shillaber with lifting the character from Smith, but he never admitted using anything but the Partington name.

Davy Jones's Locker

For over two centuries *gone to Davy Jones's locker* has been used by sailors to indicate death, especially death by drowning, but no one has yet fathomed the origins of the phrase. The words have been common at least since Tobias Smollett wrote *The Adventures of Peregrine Pickle* in 1751:

". . . I'll be damned if it was not Davy Jones himself. I know him by his saucer eyes, his three rows of teeth, and tail, and the blue smoke that came out his nostrils. . . ." This same Davy Jones, according to the mythology of sailors is the fiend that presides over all the evil spirits of the deep, and is often seen in various shapes, perching among the rigging on the eve of hurricanes, ship wrecks, and other disasters to which seafaring life is exposed, warning the devoted wretch of death and woe.

The original Davy Jones may have been the sixteenth-century owner of an English pub, commemorated in the ballad "Jones Ale Is Newe," who stored his ale in a mysterious locker for some reason much feared by seamen. Or *Jones* could be a corruption of Jonah, the unlucky biblical character swallowed by a whale, and *Davy* the Anglicization of the West Indian word *duppy*, meaning a malevolent ghost or devil. A third explanation proposes Jonah as above for *Jones*, but derives *Davy* from St. David, the patron saint of Wales often invoked by Welsh sailors. The last proposal seems best. Jonah was indeed considered bad luck to the sailors aboard the vessel on which he was attempting to flee God's wrath. And the phrase was first recorded in Captain Francis Grose's *Classical Dictionary of the Vulgar Tongue* (1785) as *David Jones' Locker*, which lends still more support to the Welsh patron saint. The *locker* in the phrase probably refers to an ordinary seaman's chest, not the old pub owner's mysterious locker.

Day of Infamy
"Yesterday, December 7, 1941, a date which will live in world history, the United States was simultaneously and deliberately attacked by naval and air forces of the Empire of Japan." So began the first draft of Franklin Delano Roosevelt's historic Pearl Harbor speech, which he wrote himself. It was only in the second draft that FDR substituted the infinitely better "infamy" for "world history" and "suddenly" for "simultaneously," making a sentence that will live in world history.

Dead as a Dodo, Dodo
The dodo left behind as its epitaph both its common name, which has become a synonym for stupidity and extinction, and its scientific name *Didus ineptus*, which says about the same for it. Barely a cen-

tury after it was discovered by man on the islands of Réunion and Mauritius, east of Madagascar, the heavy, flightless bird became extinct. Dodoes were not only big (larger than a swan), but they were barely able to run, and the colonists who settled the islands, along with their pigs, found them delicious. By the early eighteenth century the short-winged bird that seemed "to have been invented for the sole purpose of becoming extinct" was gone, leaving behind only its sad story and a synonym for something utterly extinct or a hopelessly dumb person.

Dead Sea
This salt lake in Palestine is 51 miles long and 11 miles wide, falls to a depth of about 1,300 feet and is 26 percent salt, as opposed to about 3 or 4 percent in most oceans. Because its limpid blue-green water supports practically no life, the Romans named it the *Mare Mortum*, or *Dead Sea*.

The dodo lives on only in the language.
RICHARD LYDEKKER, THE NEW NATURAL HISTORY, *1895*

To Deep-six

To *deep-six* is an old naval term meaning to drown, the *six* meaning "six fathoms down." It has since taken on the meaning of to kill a person or thing, as in "we're going to *deep-six* that project."

Devil Dogs, "Retreat, Hell!"

In World War I, the Germans called the U.S. Marines of the 4th Brigade *Teufelhunden*, or *devil dogs*, because they were such fierce fighters. The name stuck as a nickname for marines. So did the marine slogan *Retreat, hell!*, a shortening of the reply Marine Captain Lloyd Williams gave a Frenchman when asked to fall back at the Battle of Belleau Wood: "Retreat, hell! We just got here!"

To Die for the Want of Lobster Sauce

Vatel, the chef of the French Prince de Condé, is said to have killed himself because the lobsters (or fish) he needed for a sauce he was preparing for Louis XIV didn't arrive on time. Thus, *to die for the want of lobster sauce* is said of someone who suffers greatly because of some small disappointment.

Do a Brodie

The intrepid Steve Brodie once angered fighter Jim Corbett's father by publicly predicting that John L. Sullivan would knock out his son. "So you're the fellow who jumped over the Brooklyn Bridge," the elder Corbett said, when the two met for the first time shortly thereafter. "No, I jumped *off* of it," Brodie corrected him. "Oh," replied Corbett, "I thought you jumped *over* it. Any damn fool could jump off it."

As a result of his famous leap, Brodie's name became a byword—in the form of *to do* (or *pull*) *a Brodie*—for taking a great chance, even taking a suicidal leap. Brodie made his jump from the Manhattan side of the Brooklyn Bridge on July 23, 1886, to win a $200 barroom bet. Eluding guards on the bridge, the twenty-three-year-old daredevil climbed to the lowest cord and plummeted 135 feet into the water below, where friends were waiting to retrieve him in a rowboat. He was arrested for endangering his life and reprimanded by a judge, but that didn't stop him from leaping off a 212-

foot railroad bridge in Poughkeepsie, New York, two years later to win a $500 bet.

Brodie, who later became a successful saloonkeeper, always laughed at charges that he had really pushed a dummy off the Brooklyn Bridge. At any rate, his leap was not an impossible one. About ten years ago a man leaped off the George Washington Bridge from 250 feet up. He hit the water at over 70 miles an hour, and then swam two hundred yards to shore.

Dogwatch

A *dogwatch* at sea is the period between 4:00 and 6:00 P.M., the first dogwatch, or the period between 6:00 and 8:00 P.M., the second dog-watch. The other watches aboard ship are:

    12:00 to 4:00 P.M.—afternoon watch
    8:00 to 12:00 P.M.—first night watch
    12:00 to 4:00 A.M.—middle watch

The Brooklyn Bridge as it looked on completion in 1883,
when it was considered the eighth wonder of the world
VALENTINE'S MANUAL OF OLD NEW YORK

A naval action in the Spanish American War. Admiral George Dewey: "You may fire when you are ready, Gridley."

4:00 to 8:00 A.M.—morning watch
8:00 to 12:00 A.M.—forenoon watch

The dogwatches are only two hours each so that the same men aren't always on duty at the same time each afternoon. Some experts say *dogwatch* is a corruption of *dodge watch* and others associate *dogwatch* with the fitful sleep of sailors called *dog sleep,* because it is a stressful watch. But no one really knows the origin of this term, which was first recorded in 1700.

Don't Give Up the Ship
Tradition has it that Captain James Lawrence shouted these immortal words while mortally wounded when his U.S. frigate *Chesapeake* was lowering its flag in surrender to the British off Boston during the

War of 1812. He really said: "Tell the men to fire faster and not give up the ship; fight her till she sinks." Despite his order the Americans were defeated.

"Doolittle Do'd It!"

Red Skelton's "mean widdle kid" used to say "I do'd it!" on the comic's radio show in World War II days. A news story borrowed Skelton's words on April 18, 1942, when Lt. Colonel James "Jimmy" Doolittle and his men took off from the carrier *Hornet* and made the first air attack on the Japanese mainland, greatly uplifting American morale in those dark days. *"Doolittle do'd it!"* became a popular catch phrase throughout America.

Down the Hatch

Here's a drinking expression that seems to have its origins in sea freighters, where cargoes are lowered into the hatch. First used by seamen, it has only been traced back to the turn of the century.

Dreadnought

With her ten big 12-inch guns, 11-inch armor belt protection and 21.6 knot speed, the 17,940-ton British battleship *Dreadnought* outclassed any battleship on the seas and made all others virtually obsolete. Before *Dreadnought*'s 1906 debut, battleships commonly had four 12-inch guns and a number of smaller ones. The British built the *Dreadnought* in just four months, but it was three years before Germany could produce a comparable ship. The *Dreadnought* marked a turning point in naval military history and her name became the name for any big ship of comparable size. By 1916 Britain had twenty-nine dreadnoughts, enabling her to defeat Germany in the Battle of Jutland. Indeed by that time Britain had superdreadnoughts like the 27,000-ton *Warspite* with her eight 15-inch guns and 13-inch armor belt, and the original *Dreadnought* did not even see service at Jutland.

Drink Like a Fish

Fish don't intentionally drink water, of course; they get whatever water they need from their food and most of the water they appear to be drinking while swimming along is actually passing through their gills to supply them with oxygen. But they certainly do *seem* to be drinking continually, many swimming with their mouths open. That is why what has been called an "idiotism" (like "cold as hell") has been a common synonym for drinking excessively, especially alcohol, since at least the early seventeenth century. *Drunk as a fish*, which originated at about the same time, implies the same idea.

Dry Goods Stores

Dry goods stores possibly take their name from stores run by New England shipowners, many of whom were merchants in Colonial times. Their two chief imports were rum and calico, which were usually displayed on opposite sides of the store—a wet goods side containing the rum and a dry goods side holding the calico. Though "wet goods" disappeared from the language, all stores that sell yard goods are still called *dry goods stores.*

"England Expects Every Man to Do His Duty"

"England expects every man to do his duty," were Lord Nelson's famous words to his men at Trafalgar. One British member of Parliament has written that the officialese or gobbledygook so common in government services everywhere today would express the same sentiment this way: "England anticipates that, as regards the current emergency, personnel will face up to the issues and exercise appropriately the functions allocated to their respective occupational groups."

An Enoch Arden

Enoch Arden, Philip Ray and Annie Lee grew up together in a little seaport town. Though both boys loved Annie, Enoch won her hand and they lived together happily until Enoch sailed aboard the merchantman *Good Fortune* to make his fortune. Shipwrecked for ten years on a deserted island, Enoch is finally rescued. Annie, meanwhile, has been reduced to poverty and Philip asks her to marry him, certain that Enoch is dead. Enoch is brokenhearted when he returns after the ten years and witnesses, unknown to them, Annie and Philip's happiness, but he vows never to let them know of his return until after his death, sacrificing his happiness for theirs. Such is the plot of Alfred Lord Tennyson's long poem "Enoch Arden," which he based on the true story of a sailor thought drowned at sea who returned home after several years to find that his wife had remarried. A similar case was reported after the *Arctic* went down in 1854, a New Orleans merchant named Fleury believed drowned and his young widow remarrying. The "widow" had three children by her new marriage and lived happily until a letter arrived from Fleury six years later. A whaler just setting out on a long voyage had rescued him and when the whaler was also wrecked, Fleury was rescued by still another whaler starting out on a long voyage, thus accounting for the many years he had spent at sea. An *Enoch Arden* has come to mean "that rare creature who truly loves someone better than himself."

Ensign

There were no *ensigns* in the early American navy, for this only became the lowest commissioned rank in 1862. *Ensign* simply means "banner" and the first ensigns were British Army officers who led a group of men under a banner or flag.

Epsom Salts

Epsom salts take their name from the mineral springs in Epsom, England, where the natural hydrated magnesium sulfate baths attracted many people searching for good health. Seawater has essentially the same composition as *epsom salts.*

Fanny Adams, Harriet Lane

This British nautical term for stew, hash or tinned mutton is among the most gory of eponymous words. Fanny Adams was murdered and mutilated in 1812, her body cut into pieces and thrown into the River Wey at Alton in Hampshire. Her murderer, one Fred Baker, was publicly hanged in Winchester. Young Fanny's name, given wide currency, was adopted by sailors to indicate a particularly distasteful meal. Fanny Adams had been disposed of in a kettle, making the term even more apt. In fact, when kettles came into use in the British Navy they were dubbed *Fannys* from the tins before them. There is no doubt that Fanny Adams is the basis for the military expression *Sweet Fanny Adams*, meaning something worthless, or nothing at all. *Harriet Lane* is a merchant-marine term for Australian canned meat, because it supposedly resembled the chopped-up body of this girl, murdered by a man named Wainwright in about 1875.

Fata Morgana

Mirages of ships, houses and mirror images, often seen in the water as well as in the air, and often doubled—inverted above each other—have frequently been reported in the Strait of Messina and other places. They are called *fata morgana* after Morgana le Fay, a sorceress in Arthurian legend.

Father of the Waters

The American Mississippi is not the only river to have this nickname. Londoners often speak of "Father Thames" and long before them, the ancient Romans offered prayers to Father Tiber.

Fathom

Although a fathom is now a nautical measure of six feet, it was once defined by an act of Parliament as "the length of a man's arms around the object of his affections." The word derives from the Old English *faethm*, which means "the embracing arms."

Fearnought

In the nineteenth century, heavy woolen clothing worn by sailors was called *fearnought*. Seamen wearing clothing made of *fearnought* needed to "fear nought" from the weather.

Fiddler's Green

Since about 1820 British sailors have called the traditional heaven of mariners *Fiddler's Green*, "a place of unlimited rum and tobacco." Wrote Captain Frederick Marryat in his novel *Snarleyyow*:

> At Fiddler's Green, where seamen true,
> When here they've done their duty,
> The bowl of grog shall still renew,
> And pledge to love and beauty.

Figurehead

Figureheads on ships are carved figures or busts attached below the bowsprit directly over the cutwater. They are often works of art and have great ornamental value, but have no function whatsoever and ships would sail just as well without them. The carvings do inspire pride and confidence among seamen, however, and lend prestige to ships. For these reasons *figurehead* has been used for at least a century to describe a person who nominally heads an organization, who lends his good name to it but has no real duties in it.

Filibuster

Filibuster, deriving from the Dutch *vrijbuiter*, "freebooter or pirate," was originally used in American English to describe gunrunners in Central America, men who engaged in war with a country with whom their own country was at peace. The word came to mean obstruction of legislation in the U.S. Senate by prolonged speech-making when a congressman described one such obstructionist as "filibustering against the U.S."

A Fine Kettle of Fish

Ebenezer Brewer and many others claim that this expression of disgust for an awful mess (also *a pretty* or *nice kettle of fish*) has its origins in a kind of picnic held along the river Tured in the eighteenth century. The picnic was called "a kettle of fish" because salmon from the river were boiled in kettles and served to the guests, who ate them under marquees on the river bank. The negative connotation of the expression arose, the reasoning goes, because the fish were often overcooked, undercooked or seasoned

The figurehead for the U.S. Navy frigate Lancaster *was carved by marine John Haley Bellamy, America's leading artist in wood, early in the 1880s. The huge gilded eagle weighs over one and a half tons and its wing span is eighteen feet.*

THE MARINER'S MUSEUM

69

improperly; that the kettle of fish frequently spilled over; or that eating the fish was messy—any or all of these situations giving rise to our term for a mess, or muddle. These fêtes champêtres or "kettles of fish" *were* held, but that is the only evidence linking them to the expression.

Just as good an explanation is found in the English word *kiddle*. A *kiddle* or *kiddle net* is a basket set in the sluiceways of dams to catch fish, a device well known from the time of the Plantagenets. Royal officials had the perquisite to trap fish in kiddles, but poachers often raided the traps of fish, frequently destroying the kiddles in the process. Possibly an official came upon a destroyed trap and exclaimed, "That's a pretty kiddle of fish!" or something similar, meaning "a pretty sorry state of affairs!" and the phrase was born. Repeated over the years, *kiddle* was corrupted in everyday speech to *kettle*, giving us the expression as we know it today.

Finnan Haddie

Haddock gives us the *haddie* for this fish dish, while the *Finnan* comes from either the River Findhorn or the village of Findon, both, of course, in Scotland.

First-rate, Second-rate, Third-rate . . .

Starting in Elizabethan times and up until the nineteenth century, British warships were rated by the number of guns they carried and the weight of those guns, rather than by the weight of the ships themselves. Six rates or categories were applied, a mighty first-rate ship being the highest of them. Before long these technical naval terms were being used to describe degrees of excellence generally, as in 1681, when we find an English author noting, "There are your first, second, third, fourth and fifth-rate wits, too."

Fishfall, Frogfall

Fishfalls, or a rain of fish falling from the sky, have occurred fairly often throughout the world, probably due to waterspouts that suck up fish and water and release them miles away. Similarly, *frogfalls* are common phenomena, too.

To Fish in Troubled Waters

This old saying means "to take advantage of another's marital troubles to gain something for yourself." It refers to the fact that fish bite best in rough waters, as all good fishermen know.

Fish Names from Other Animals

Many fish are named after animals, including: alligator, bird, boar, buffalo, cat, dog, elephant, frog, goat, goose, hawk, horse, leopard, lizard, parrot, porcupine, rabbit, robin, sheep, squirrel, tiger, toad, unicorn, viper, wolf and zebra fishes. How many more can you add to the list?

Fish or Cut Bait

A demand that someone should take a definite stand, take action instead of procrastinating, or else stop trying and give somebody else a chance to act. The American expression has been associated with politics since Joseph "Uncle Joe" Cannon first used it in a speech in Congress on August 5, 1876, while upbraiding the Demo-

The porcupine fish, one of many sea creatures named for other animals

LOUIS FIGUER, THE OCEAN WORLD, *1896*

71

crats on the other side of the House, but it is almost certainly much older. Someone in a choice fishing spot on land or aboard a ship was possibly told to stop fooling around, to either drop his line in the water and fish, or cut the bait from his line and let another fisherman take his place. Another explanation points to commercial fishing vessels. Cutting bait fish into chum, or bait, is the duty of one or more crew members on such ships. One either fished or cut bait on these vessels and in time this practice led to the expression *fish or cut bait*—make a choice or take a stand—even though fishermen were usually *told* whether they would fish or cut bait.

Fishy Sayings

A fish out of water: One who is awkward and out of his usual surroundings.
A loose fish: A person of loose or dissolute habits.
A pretty kettle of fish: (see page 69)
A queer fish: An eccentric.

He eats no fish: A non-Catholic in Elizabethan times.

I have other fish to fry: I'm busy; I can't do anything else right now.

Neither fish, flesh, nor fowl: Suitable to no class of people; neither the clergy, who eat fish, nor the generality, who eat flesh, nor the poor, who eat fowl.

The best fish swim near the bottom: Anything worthwhile takes trouble to obtain.

There's as good fish in the sea as ever came out of it: Don't be discouraged if you lose one chance; there will be another just as good.

To drink like a fish: (see page 63)

To feed the fishes: To drown.

To fish for compliments: To try to obtain praise by posing leading questions.

To fish in troubled waters: (see page 71)

Fish or cut bait: (see page 71)

Fjord

Any long, narrow arm of the sea running up between high banks or cliffs is called a *fjord* or *fiord*, a word with prehistoric origins. Usually formed by glacial erosion, these inlets are particularly common in Norway, where a *fjord* can also be "a bay."

Flamingo

Spanish explorers in the New World named this long-legged pink wading bird, which eats with its head upside down in the water, for the people of Flanders, the *Flemings*, as they were called. Flemings were widely known for their lively personalities, flushed complexions and their love of bright, gay clothing. The Spaniards thought it was a great joke naming the bird the *flamingo*, which means "a Fleming" in Spanish and became the English *flamingo* in time.

Flatboats, Kentucky Arks, Keelboats and Store Boats

Adam Gimbel, founder of the great Gimbels department-store chain, among other pioneer American merchants, often fitted out *flatboats* with shelves and counters, stocked them with goods and floated downriver to sell his wares on the banks of towns too small to have permanent stores. Such early American *store boats* stocked anything from groceries to dry goods, liquor and gunpowder. Many flew light calico flags and at the end of each spring trip, the boats were taken apart downstream and sold for lumber. Sometimes the merchants used *keelboats* instead of the *flatboats* or *Kentucky arks*. Keelboats were better made and could travel upstream, being propelled by oars, poles, sails or a team of mules towing from along the bank. Intense rivalry between crews of these two types of riverboat led to bitter fights on the river that made the boats unwelcome in many towns, but both flatboats and keelboats were of great importance in developing the American west.

Quaint fishing villages dot the rugged coastline on a Norwegian fjords cruise aboard a modern luxury liner.
RoyaL Viking Line, Inc.

Flattop

A converted coal ship, the *Langley*, commissioned in 1922, was America's first aircraft carrier. But no one thought of calling any aircraft carrier a *flattop* until World War II, when the United States built 150 carriers. The planes launched from them destroyed 527 enemy ships and 12,000 planes.

Flemish

To *flemish* rope, which is done only after a boat is secured, is to coil it down concentrically in the direction of the sun or like the coil of a watch spring, beginning in the center. *Flemish* also once meant "to force or score the planks." The terms seem to have arisen in the early nineteenth century and take their name from Flemish sailors, considered to be neat seamen and who may have coiled their rope like this.

Flotsam and Jetsam; Lagan; Findals

These words were once distinctly different legal terms for wreckage found in the sea. While *flotsam*, from the Old French *floter* (Latin *fluere*), "to float," meant the goods or parts of a wreck found floating on the sea and belonged to the Crown, *jetsam*, which could be claimed by the lord of the manor, derived from the French *jeter* (Latin *jacere*), "to throw out," meant cargo or equipment purposely thrown overboard, or jettisoned, in order to lighten a ship in an emergency. Jetsam could only be considered flotsam if it was found between the high and low waterlines, because no one could tell if it had been jettisoned there or had floated there. As for *lagan*, it referred to jetsam lying at the bottom of the sea but which was usually marked with a buoy in order to be found again by the ship's owners. *Any* goods found in the sea were called *findals*, including an abandoned ship, or derelict. We rarely use any of these terms today. The metaphor *flotsam and jetsam* is used mainly in clichés such as "the flotsam and jetsam of life," the remains of the human shipwrecks life makes.

Flying Dutchman

One superstition has it that any mariner who sees the *Flying Dutchman* will die within the day. The tale of the *Flying Dutchman* trying to round the Cape of Good Hope against strong winds and never succeeding, then trying to make Cape Horn and failing there too, has been the most famous of maritime ghost stories for over three hundred years. The cursed spectral ship sailing back and forth on its endless voyage, its ancient white-haired crew crying for help while hauling at her sails, inspired Samuel Taylor Coleridge to write his classic "The Rime of the Ancient Mariner," to name but one famous literary work. The real *Flying Dutchman* is supposed to have set sail in 1660.

Forecastle (Fo'c'sle)
By the fourteenth century the forward part of many large ships had an area that was raised and protected like a castle from which the captain commanded the decks of an enemy. Today the forecastle is simply "that part of the upper deck forward of the foremast or, in merchant ships, the forward part of the vessel under the deck, where the sailors live." *Forecastle* is almost always spelled and pronounced *fo'c'sle* (fo'ksl).

Founder
A ship that *founders* fills with water and goes to the *bottom*. I emphasize *bottom* because this is the key to the ancestry of the word *founder*, which comes from the Latin *fundus*, meaning "bottom."

Franklin's Gull
The only bird ever to have a monument erected to it, this black-headed gull was named in honor of Sir John Franklin (1786–1847), the English explorer who died in discovering the Northwest Passage that so many other mariners had striven to find. *Franklin's gull* (*Larus pipixan*) is perhaps the most prominent bird in American folklore. In 1848 an invasion of grasshoppers threatened starvation for the Mormon settlers near the Great Salt Lake and it was checked only by the appearance of flocks of *Franklin's gulls* that devoured the crickets and saved the crops after all other means had failed. The Sea Gull Monument on Temple Square in Salt Lake City is dedicated to the species, "in grateful remembrance of the mercy of God to the Mormon pioneers."

Fudge

No one knows the origins of *fudge candy*, but Isaac D'Israeli, father of the British prime minister, had an interesting story about the word *fudge* for lies or nonsense. Wrote D'Israeli in his *Curiosities of Literature* (1791): "There was sir, in our time one Captain Fudge, commander of a merchantman, who upon his return from a voyage, how ill-fraught soever his ship was, always brought home a good cargo of lies, so much that now aboard ship the sailors, when they hear a great lie told, cry out, 'You fudge it!'" D'Israeli probably wasn't *fudging*, because a notorious liar named Captain Fudge, called "Lying Fudge," did live in seventeenth-century England. His name, possibly in combination with the German word *futch*, "no good," may well be the source of the word *fudge*.

Full Nelson

All the wrestling holds and falls known today were depicted on the walls of the Egyptian tombs of Beni Hassan three thousand years or more ago, so the earliest wrestlers must have employed some form of the many variations on the *full nelson*. But the term didn't come into use until the nineteenth century, when it was named either for some celebrated grappler who excelled at the pressure hold, or for *Nelson*, a town in Lancashire, England, once famous for its wrestling matches. The town of Nelson changed its name from Marston in the nineteenth century, calling itself after the popular *Lord Nelson Inn* there, which in turn honored England's great naval hero. So if the town Nelson is responsible for the hold's name, the hold can also be said to honor the great Horatio.

Gabriel's Hounds

Gabriel's hounds are wild geese, so called because their sound in flight is like a pack of hounds in full cry. Legend has it that they are the souls of unbaptized children wandering in space until the day of judgment.

Gangplank, Gangboard

Whether it's called a *gangplank* or *gangboard*, the plank connecting a ship to land takes its name from the Old English *gang*, a way or passage, because it was a way of going on or off a ship. It was named long before *gang* acquired its present meaning.

Gangway

On ancient galleys the *gangboard*, deriving from *gang*, was the narrow boardwalk the rowers walked down to pass from stem to stern. *Gangboard* then became the board with railings that passengers use on entering or exiting a ship, the word becoming *gangway* in time.

Gefilte Fish

Hot or cold it is delicious, but the Jewish delicacy, made with many ingredients and traditionally served on Friday nights, is *not* a separate species of fish. *Gefilte fish* is a kind of fish loaf made of various ground fish, eggs, onions, pepper, salt and sometimes sugar—every good cook having her or his secret ingredients or method. The Yiddish word derives from the German for "stuffed fish."

To Get a Rise out of Someone

When these words were first used they applied to fish rising to the bait. Izaak Walton and other writers on the art of angling popularized the word *rise* in this sense three hundred years ago, and the metaphor from fly-fishing became standard English. Just as the fish rises to the bait and is caught, the person who rises to the lure of a practical joke becomes the butt of it. From its original meaning of raising a laugh at someone's expense, the words have been extended to include the idea of attracting attention in general—getting a rise out of a sales prospect, et cetera.

Give a Man Luck and Throw Him in the Sea

A man with luck will survive anything. The old saying brings to mind Jonah, who was thrown into the sea and swallowed by a whale, only to escape, and Arion, who was thrown into the sea and brought to shore by a dolphin.

Give a Whaling To

Many etymologists believe this phrase should be *give a waling to*, as a *wale* is a mark raised on the flesh by the blow of a stick or whip. But the key word in the phrase has been spelled with an *h* ever since it first appeared two centuries ago. This suggests that a *whaling*, "a terrible beating," was one given with a whalebone whip or, possibly, that the whalebone whip and the wales it raised both contributed to the phrase, making it more vivid. Riding whips were commonly made of whalebone in the eighteenth and nineteenth centuries and were used to beat more than horses. Whalebone, incidentally, is a misnomer: It's not made from the bones of a whale but from a substance found in the whale's upper jaw.

Give a Wide Berth To

At least since the early seventeenth century, *berth*, its origin unknown, has meant working or operating room for a ship. *Giving good berth* to a ship, the earliest version of this nautical expression, meant to avoid or keep far away from her, which is what *give a wide berth to* means today, in reference to ships or anything else.

Gob

Back in the twenties the U.S. Navy banned the use of *gob* for a sailor, claiming it was undignified. Like most such comstockery, the ban on *gob* failed, but the Navy might have been right about its dignity, considering the word's possible origins. *Gob*, first recorded in 1909, probably comes from either *gobble*, an allusion to the way many sailors were reputed to eat, or from the word *gob* for spit, in reference to English coast guardsmen who were called *gobbies* in the past because they were in the habit of expectorating so much. Little better is the suggestion that the word is from the Irish *gob*, "mouth," as in the expression *shut your gob*. Sailors might then have been compared to "big mouths" or something similar.

To Go by the Board

This expression, originating in England, literally means to go overboard, to fall down past the *board*, or side of a ship, into the sea. Since the mid-eighteenth century it has also figuratively meant to be utterly lost, as in the first recorded use of the expression: "Every instinct and feeling of humanity goes by the board."

Gondolas

The small American *gondolas* of the Revolutionary War take their name from the Italian double-ended boats used on the Grand Canal in Venice, but there the resemblance ends. The Continental gondolas were rigged with sails and fitted with guns. The most famous of them was the *Philadelphia* (1776), built by hero-traitor Benedict Arnold as part of an eight-gondola flotilla that frustrated Britain's first major effort to divide and subdue her rebellious American colonies at the Battle of Valcour Island. Sunk during the war and raised in 1935, she is now at the Smithsonian Institution and is the oldest intact man-of-war presently exhibited in North America.

To Go (in) Off the Deep End

These words were suggested by someone leaping off the diving board at the deep end of a swimming pool and finding the water was

The continental gondola Philadelphia, *the oldest intact man-of-war in North America*

over his head. When first used, as military slang in England during World War I, they simply meant to get very excited, as if finding yourself in deep water. Then they came to mean "passionate" as well. An English novelist wrote: "In her set the word adultery was not often mentioned. One went in off the deep end about somebody. . . ." American use of the expression is often similar, but we also apply it to other situations. Someone who displays a terrible temper, or is so reckless that he has gone into a situation over his head, or even someone who is crazy is said *to have gone off the deep end.*

Grable-Bodied Seamen
Movie actress Betty Grable, her "million-dollar legs" insured by Lloyds of London, was the pin-up girl par excellence during World War II. British sailors used the term *Grable-bodied seamen* to describe long-stemmed lovelies in the Wrens (Women's Royal Naval Service) who fit the description. Miss Grable, born in St. Louis, Missouri, in 1916 married bandleader Harry James, who died in 1983.

Greek Fire
Greek fire, the mysterious ancient naval weapon that burned when wet and was so effective against wooden ships from A.D. 700–900, is said to have been invented by the Greek Callimachus. No one knows its constituents, but it is thought to have been composed of sulfur, naphtha and pitch. Water helped *Greek fire* spread and it could only be extinguished with wine.

Greenacre
When they hanged James Greenacre at Newgate prison in 1837 the rope broke. But no sympathy was shown for the murderer, who had cut up his victim and buried parts of the woman in different sites of London. Stevedores, in fact, promptly adopted the killer's name to indicate the falling of cargo. Whenever rope slings broke while goods were being loaded or unloaded, the cry *Greenacre!* could be heard along the docks.

Grog

The War of Jenkins's Ear (see page 210) made Admiral Sir Edward Vernon England's hero of the hour in 1739. Parliament voted him formal thanks and street pageants were held on his birthday to celebrate his humbling of the Spaniards. Some of his officers remembered "Old Grog," too; George Washington's half brother, Lawrence, named Mount Vernon after him, but the arrogant old war hawk never won popularity with his men. Old Grog had been nicknamed for the impressive grogram cloak he wore on deck in all kinds of weather, the coarse taffeta material symbolizing his tough and irascible nature. Then, in 1740, the stern disciplinarian issued an order that made his name a malediction. In order to curb drunken brawling aboard ships in his command, he declared that all rum rations would henceforth be diluted with water. Incensed old sea dogs cursed Vernon roundly, for half a pint of rum mixed with a quart of water seemed weak stuff indeed to anyone on a raw rum diet. Furthermore, the rationed bilge was divided into two issues served six hours apart. His men soon defiantly dubbed the adulterated rum *grog*, using the nickname they had bestowed upon the admiral. Vernon's orders served its purpose and "three water rum" became the official ration for all enlisted personnel in the Royal Navy, but *grog* quickly took on the wider meaning of any cheap, diluted drink. Eventually, *grog* came to mean liquor itself, diluted or not, and it was either a little stronger *grog* or a lot of the weaker concoction that made one unsteady on one's feet and resulted in the pugilistic and now general *groggy*. Admiral Vernon, of course, never imagined that he would be remembered for anything but his victories. Old Grog continued to serve in his usual belligerent, eccentric way. But he went too far. In 1746, when sixty-two years old, he was dismissed from the Royal Navy for writing pamphlets attacking the Admiralty. He spent his last eleven years on land cursing and grumbling about his fate.

Guinea Pig

Here is a rat relative that is named after a ship. This South American rodent isn't a pig, doesn't look like a pig and doesn't hail from Guinea in West Africa. Native to Brazil, it takes its first name from the fact that it was first brought to Europe on the *Guinea-men* slave ships that sailed from Guinea to South America to deliver their human cargo and filled their holds with whatever cargo was available for the return trip to Europe. How the creature was mistaken for a pig is anybody's guess. Our slang expression *guinea pig* for anyone who is used to test something obviously derives from the widespread use of the guinea pig in scientific experiments.

Gunboat Diplomacy

Gunboat, for a small ship fitted with guns, can be traced back to 1793, but we don't have a printed reference to *gunboat diplomacy*, which might translate as "getting one's way by force," until 1927. The expression may, however, date back to 1841, when American ships exacted trade concessions from the Chinese by sending gunboats to Canton, a few years after the British had done the same in the First Opium War.

Gung Ho

In Chinese *gung ho* means "work together," but after Carlson's Raiders, the 2nd Marine Raider Division commanded by Lt. Colonel Evans F. Carlson, a veteran of the China campaign, adopted the expression as their slogan in World War II, it took on a different meaning. Carlson's Raiders, who made daring raids on Guadalcanal and other Japanese strongholds, were a remarkably brave, loyal and enthusiastic band, so *gung ho* came to describe these qualities. Yet when noncombat marines and soldiers displayed the same enthusiasm in picayune matters such as white-glove inspections and policing for cigarette butts, *gung ho* was disparagingly applied to them, resulting in its present meaning of an overzealous person.

Guppy Submarine

Next to the goldfish the *guppy*, or "rainbow fish" (*Lebistes reticulatus*), also called the millions fish, is the best known of home aquarium fish. Guppies take their name from R. J. Lechmere Guppy, once president of the Scientific Association of Trinidad, who presented the British Museum with specimens of the species in the late nineteenth century. Numerous in South America, they devour mosquito larvae and so help to prevent malaria. A namesake of the guppy is the streamlined *guppy submarine*, developed toward the end of World War II. The sub's name is also an acronym, the first four letters standing for "*g*reater *u*nderwater *p*ropulsion *p*ower."

Halcyon Days

After a storm shipwrecked and killed her mortal husband, the heart-broken goddess Alcyone, daughter of Aeolus, the wind god of Greek legend, drowned herself in the sea. Punishing the suicide, the angry gods turned both Alcyone and her husband, Ceyx, into birds later known as halcyons, or kingfishers as we call them today. Yet the goddess's father took pity on the couple and decreed that during the halcyon's breeding season, the seven days before and the seven days after the shortest day of the year, the sea would always be perfectly calm and unruffled. Thus, during the fourteen days, at about the time of the winter solstice, the halcyons could sit on their nests, which floated securely on the tranquil water, borne by currents across the world, hatching their eggs.

This legend was widely believed through Roman times, when Alcyone's name became Halcyone, and well into the fifteenth century. The *halcyon days* had an actual place on ancient calendars and the legend inspired much poetry, including Percy Bysshe Shelley's famous: "The halcyons brood around the formless isles,/The treacherous ocean has foresworn its wiles." Kingfishers were also believed to be able to predict the weather, and stuffed specimens, wings outstretched, were even used as weather vanes. Eventually, all the legends and the exquisitely peaceful sound of the word *halcyon* (hal-see-un) itself made the phrase *halcyon days* mean not only windless days of peace and calm, but any time of peace, serenity and rejoicing.

Half-seas Over

American colonists had many synonyms for *drunk*—so many, in fact, that Benjamin Franklin published a list of 228 such terms, com-

The halibut, a truly "holy" fish
LOUIS FIGUER, THE OCEAN WORLD, *1896*

plete with rarities like *nimptopsicall, cherry-merry* and *loose in the hilt.* Some of these words and phrases, many borrowed from other countries, live on today, including *half-seas over*, a person quite drunk but not yet under the table. British in origin and dating back to the late seventeenth century, the words probably originated in the resemblance of a drunk's walk to a man walking the deck of a storm-battered ship, one side heeled over in the sea. Either the expression was fathered by this *half-seas over*, or it is a corruption of *op-zee-zober* ("oversea beer"), a strong heady beer imported from Holland in the seventeenth century. The earlier phrase *halfway across the sea* for a drunk suggests that the former theory is correct.

Halibut
In Old English every flatfish from the flounder to the skate was called a *butt*, even the largest of the flounders, *Hippoglossus hippoglossus*, which often weighed four hundred pounds, and measured eight feet in length. So esteemed was *Hippoglossus* five centuries or so ago that the "hallowed giant of all the demersal species" was eaten only on Church holy days and became known as the *haly*

("holy") *butt.* This fish is no longer reserved for holy days, of course, but it is still known as the *halibut* or "holy flounder."

Hand over Fist

Rapid ascent into the rigging on old sailing ships was made by climbing hand over hand up a thick rope—a skill sailors prided themselves on—and when sails were hoisted, the same *hand over hand* technique prevailed, just as it did when ropes or even fish were hauled in. In about the nineteenth century, American seamen changed this expression to the more descriptive *hand over fist*, which shows one fist clenching a rope and a loose hand passing over it to make another fist on the rope, et cetera. The sense of hauling in and rapid ascent on the ropes soon suggested someone rising rapidly in the business world and hauling in money, which is what we still mean when we say someone is making money *hand over fist*.

Happy as a Clam at High Tide, Close as a Clam, Clam Up

Since clams are usually dug at low tide, a clam might be happy indeed at high tide. This expression is an Americanism first noted in 1834. *Close as a clam*, describing a stingy person, refers to the difficulty in opening a clam shell and is an older expression that probably originated in England. *Clam up*, however, is an Americanism for "to become silent, refuse to disclose information," dating back to 1916 and referring again to the difficulty of opening the "lips" of the clam. *Clam* for "mouth" has been common in America since the early nineteenth century.

Hardtack

Tack, over a century ago, meant food of any kind. Seamen took to calling hard biscuit—biscuit that was hard and lasted long voyages in rough weather—*hard tack*, or what we'd more often call *dog biscuits* today.

Hard Up

Hard up the helm! was the order given at sea when the weather was bad and the tiller had to be put up as far as possible to the windward in order to turn the ship's head away from the wind. This term came to mean "to weather the storm as best you can" and then took on the meaning of being short of money—that is, the condition of someone weathering a storm.

Hell Afloat, Prison Ships

British prison ships, usually old hulks no good for sailing anymore, were the concentration camps of the Revolutionary War. It has been estimated that they took the lives of more American fighting men (11,000 to 15,000) during the Revolution than enemy rifles did. The *Whitby*, the first such infamous ship, stripped of her fittings and her gunports nailed securely, was anchored in Wallabout Bay, off Brooklyn, New York. Such ships were often dubbed *hell afloat* by the prisoners, whatever the ship's real name.

Hell Gate

Before this famous narrow passage in New York Harbor was blasted, thousands of vessels were wrecked against the rocks in its strong, conflicting currents. Dutch mariners in early New York probably named it so, calling it *Hel Gat*, though some etymologists have suggested that it derives from the Dutch for "whirling gut."

Hell's Bells!

Originating in the late nineteenth century, this imprecation was born at sea, being a shortening of the more colorful curse *Hell's bells and buckets of blood!*

The High Seas, the Main

The high seas, or the "main," are the open seas—those waters beyond any territorial limit that belong to no one nation. *High* in the term *high seas* means "chief" or "principal."

Hippopotamus

The *hippopotamus* was named by the Greeks, who somehow thought it looked like a horse and, since it spent so much time in the water, called it "river horse," from the Greek *hippos*, "horse," and

*A British prison ship off New York during the Revolution-
ary War*

potamos, "river." Wrote the British historian Thomas Macaulay, "I have seen the Hippo both asleep and awake, and I can assure you that, asleep or awake, he is the ugliest of the Works of God."

Hobsonize

To kiss, from the only person in history whose name the dictionaries immortalize in this way. Lieutenant Richmond Pearson Hobson (1870–1937) won fame during the Spanish-American War, stepping into the national limelight when he tried to sink the collier *Merrimac* and block Santiago Harbor. No matter that Hobson and his seven men failed on that morning of June 3, 1898—a Spanish shell hit the steering gear and their ship sank in a broad part of the channel where it couldn't prevent Admiral Pascual Cervara's squadron from leaving—because other tactics were employed and the entire Spanish fleet was destroyed at the battle of Santiago a month later. Hobson, a handsome Annapolis graduate—known there as "The Parson" for his religious fervor—became a hero for leading the daring early morning mission.

The young naval engineer was honored with parades and dinners wherever he went when he returned to the United States in August 1898. His good looks and popularity led to his name becoming a verb meaning *to kiss*: women often flung their arms around him and showered him with kisses when he appeared in public. "Kissing Bug Hobson," as he was called, resigned from the Navy and ran for Congress back home in Alabama, a state that later gave us another osculatory politician, Governor "Kissin' Jim" Folsom. At any rate, the hero got himself easily elected, serving from 1907 to 1915. Hobson adopted the prohibition cause, advocated naval expansion and lectured around the country. Though *hobsonize* is an obsolete expression today, it remains in historical dictionaries as one of the most curious of linguistic curiosities.

The Hogging Moment

Any time a ship is out of the water at both ends and waterborne amidships is known as *the hogging moment.* The opposite moment of stress is called *the sagging moment.*

Indian fisherman often netted rather than hooked fish
LIBRARY OF CONGRESS

Holystone

Soft sandstone, often used to scrub the decks of ships, is called holystone because it is full of holes. First it had the name *holeystone*, losing the *e*, it is said, because sailors who used it knew no ease (*E's*) and had to kneel as if in prayer (a holy attitude) when scrubbing the decks.

Hook, Line and Sinker; Hooks

An extremely gullible person who swallows a fantastic yarn or lie *hook, line and sinker* is like a hungry fish who gulps down not only the fisherman's baited hook, but the line beneath the hook and the line's weight or sinker as well. The Americanism has been traced back to the age of Davy Crockett, when tall tales hooked many a fish hungry for belief. But a sixteenth-century British expression, *to swallow a gudgeon* (a small bait fish), conveyed the same idea. No one knows for sure, but before fishing hooks were invented, early man may have used nets, traps, clubs, spears, harpoons and the bow and arrow to catch fish. Fishing hooks and line do date back at least to Mesolithic times (a transitional period between the Paleolithic and Neolithic ages), as the remains of many early bone fishhooks in the Baltic area indicate. Metal hooks made their first appearance with the coming of metal during Neolithic times.

Hooker

Some authorities say that *hooker*, for a prostitute, is so named for a line of small vessels called hookers that traded between British ports and the Hook of Holland in the nineteenth century. Ladies of the night, it is said, would wait at the Hook for sailors from the hookers and lure them to their rooms.

Horse Latitudes

These regions of calms, found at 30° N and S latitudes, may be so named because sailing ships carrying horses to America became becalmed and had to throw horses overboard in order to lighten the vessels and to take advantage of any slight breeze that did blow up. Yet the name may simply be a translation of *golfo de las yeguas*, "gulf of the mares," which was the Spanish name for the ocean between Spain and the Canary Islands and compares the supposed fickleness of mares with the fickle winds in these latitudes.

Hunky-dory

No one is certain but there may be nautical roots attached to this nineteenth-century term meaning OK or all right. *Hunk* was the word for home base in a game of the time, and the *dory* in the expression may allude to the fabled seaworthiness of the famous fisherman's dory. In any case, there have been no better suggestions.

Hurricane

Deriving from the Spanish *huracán*, a *hurricane* was first a violent tropical cyclonic storm of the western North Atlantic, but it came to mean a violent storm in general. A hurricane is called a hurricane in the Caribbean Sea, but a cyclone in the Indian Ocean, and a typhoon in the China Sea.

Hydroplane

Almost as soon as the airplane became a reality in the early twentieth century, inventors began experimenting with seaplanes with floats that were able to take off from and land on the sea. These were called *hydroplanes* and some of the first examples were built in France. But the name created some confusion, and still does, for it had, since 1870, been used as the name for a light, high-powered boat designed to plane over the water at high speeds. Invented by English pastor Charles Meade Ramus in the mid-nineteenth century, the hydroplane boat did not become a reality until about the same time as the seaplane. It is often called the *sea sled* or *hydrofoil* today.

DILIGENZA DI RITORNO DALLA LUNA

*An Italian artist's conception of a flying ship returning
from the moon with captives*

LIBRARY OF CONGRESS

95

The Ice Bear, Winter Bear

The *ice bear* is a name that Eskimos give to a monstrous grizzly bear that they fear even more than the polar bear. In the course of roaming about the country, these grizzlies sometimes take a dip in the water and roll in the snow, their fur becoming thickly coated with ice. From time immemorial the Eskimos have feared this deadly *winter bear*, for the thick ice serves as a shield that breaks any arrows shot at it and has been known to stop bullets.

A nineteenth-century print shows a polar bear on an ice ledge as sailors kill walruses in the background
LIBRARY OF CONGRESS

96

"Sir, I Have Not Yet Begun to Fight!"

Did John Paul Jones say this during the famous battle between the *Bonhomme Richard* and the *Serapis*? It seems that some of Jones's men cried for surrender, but the captain laid one of them low with the side of his pistol, fracturing his skull. Surrender? Not John Paul Jones! Captain Richard Pearson of the *Serapis* then asked Jones if he had had enough. Jones uttered the immortal words: "Sir, I have not yet begun to fight!" So, at least, Lieutenant Richard Dale later recalled; Jones himself claimed that he answered Pearson's query with the far less colorful words "I have not yet thought of it, but am determined to make you strike." There is a Marine Corps story that an American marine firing away from one of the fighting tops when he heard "I have not yet begun to fight!" turned to his companion and said: "There's always some damned fool who doesn't get the word!"

I'm All Right, Jack

Dating back at least to the late nineteenth century, when it is first recorded, *I'm all right, Jack*, was originally British naval slang employing the *Jack* of *Jack Tar* (see page 100) and a shortening of the lustier "F--- you, I'm all right, Jack" common in the ranks at the time.

Impressment, Press Gangs

Though recorded as early as 1787, *impressment* became prominent in American vocabularies before the War of 1812, when British sailors forcibly removed British seamen from American vessels, claiming this was their right, and impressed American seamen into British service at the same time, always explaining later that they took the Americans by mistake. *Press gangs* were the hired thugs who impressed seamen for service aboard British ships during the War of 1812 and had indeed done so since the late seventeenth century.

In a Pretty Pickle; Pickle

In de pikel zitten, a Dutch phrase going back at least four centuries, literally means to sit in the salt solution used for preserving pickles. This saying apparently suggested the expression to be *in a pretty pickle*, an uncomfortable or sorry plight—like someone sitting in such a bath. Our word *pickle* also comes from the Dutch. A sour pickle is the last thing anyone would expect to be named after a man, but at least one source claims that the word *pickle* derives from the name of a William Beukel or Bukelz, a fourteenth-century Dutchman who supposedly pickled the first fish, inventing the process by which we shrink and sour cucumbers. This pickled herring theory may be a red herring, however. All the big dictionaries follow the *Oxford English Dictionary*'s lead in tracing pickle to the medieval Dutch word *pekel*, whose origin is ultimately unknown. Beukel does seem very similar to *pekel*, though.

In the Doghouse
The expression *in the doghouse*, out of favor or undergoing punishment, isn't of ancient origin, but is an Americanism first recorded toward the end of the nineteenth century. Possibly the term originated during the African slave trade, when sailors locked the hatches at night, to prevent slaves from escaping, and slept on deck in tiny sleeping cubicles called "doghouses." There is no evidence, however, to support this theory, or any other for that matter.

In the Doldrums
Doldrums has come to mean any area where a ship is likely to be becalmed, especially that area near the equator noted for calms between the northeast and southeast trade winds. *Doldrums* itself probably derives from the words *dull* and tan*trum*, as if the dullness of such an area could drive one to tantrums. The expression *in the doldrums* means "down in the dumps," much like mariners felt when they weren't moving anywhere.

Irish Pennants
Nautical slang often reflects hostility toward particular groups of people. This is the case with *Irish pennants*, which originated as British naval slang for untidy ropes hanging from the rigging aloft. In another age, when the Dutch were England's major foes on the high seas, *Dutch pennants* meant the same thing.

Ishmael

"Call me Ishmael" begins Herman Melville's *Moby-Dick*, probably the most familiar opening sentence in American literature. An *Ishmael* is an outcast, which is one reason why Melville gave the name to his narrator. Ishmael was the son of Abraham and Hagar; he and his mother were banished to the wilderness by Sarah, where an angel predicted that he would forever be at odds with society (Genesis 21:9–21). The Muslims, however, do not share this biblical tradition, considering Ishmael their progenitor.

Isinglass

Derived from the Dutch *huizenblas,* "sturgeon's bladder," *isinglass* is a semitransparent substance made from that fish's bladder. Isinglass is still employed in cooking as a form of gelatin used as a thickening agent, though it was once much more popular. It also served as a substitute glass in some cases, even for windshields on early roadsters.

It's All Plain Sailing

Plane sailing in technical nautical parlance means determining a ship's position on the assumption that the earth is flat and the ship is on a plane; this is a simple, straightforward method of computing distances. In the nineteenth century the words entered general use as an expression meaning "perfectly straightforward action, a course of action that there need be no hesitation about." But the word *plane* came to be spelled *plain* and has remained that way ever since, even though it is wrong.

Jack Tar, an Old Tar, Jack

According to one story, sailors in Lord Nelson's navy wore overalls and broad-brimmed hats made of the tar-impregnated tarpaulin cloth commonly used aboard ship. The hats, and the sailors who wore them, were called *tarpulins*, which was finally shortened to *tars.* The term *Jack* has been common for a sailor at least since the mid-seventeenth century, and *Jack Tar* became the name for a British sailor. Another authority, however, believes that the name *Jack Tar* arose in the seventeenth century, when sailors wore canvas

Jack Tars of the nineteenth century

breeches that were often spotted with the tar from the waterproofing they did aboard ship. There is a reference to *Jack Tars* in William Congreve's *Love for Love* (1695), which seems to support the latter theory.

Jacob's Ladder

A ship's wood-runged rope or chain ladder primarily used to let people ascend from or descend to smaller boats alongside is called a *Jacob's ladder.* But so is a steep flight of steps up a cliff, an herb or flower formed like a ladder, and a burglar's ladder. All take their name from the ladder seen by the biblical patriarch Jacob in a vision (Genesis 28: 12–13):

> And he dreamed, behold a ladder set up on the earth, and the top of it reached to heaven: and behold the angels of God ascending and descending on it.
> And, behold, the LORD stood above it. . . .

The ladder in the dream symbolizes the hopes of Jacob for his descendants.

The Jamestown Ships

Three small ships—the *Susan Constant*, 100 tons; the *Godspeed*, 40 tons; and the *Discovery*, 20 tons—are called the *Jamestown ships* because they brought Captain John Smith and English colonists to Jamestown, Virginia, in 1607 to form the first English settlement in America. Exact replicas of these ships can be seen today at Festival Park in Jamestown, which has been called the "birthplace of the United States."

Jane, *or* Jane's

Often heard referred to as an authority in arguments about warships, *Jane* or *Jane's* simply refers to the prime reference on the world's navies, *Jane's Fighting Ships*, an illustrated book published periodically in England.

Jaunty

Jaunty has its origins in the attitude of sailors entitled to brandish a whip. Any *jaunty* person, one who swaggers about cocksurely, takes the adjective describing him from the *jaunty* or master-at-arms aboard British naval ships who supervised floggings. This jaunty in turn took his name from a mispronunciation of the French *gendarme* or policeman.

Jenny Haniver

Ancient mariners believed, like P. T. Barnum, that there should be "poetic license in mermaids." Sailors of old sometimes fashioned strange figures from dried skates, rays or mantas they had caught.

Replicas of the little ships that brought colonists to Jamestown in 1607 are now on display there
JAMESTOWN, YORKTOWN FOUNDATION

Gullible landlubbers often bought these "mermaids" and "dragons," believing them to be real. Beginning in the thirteenth century, sailors turned out such *Jenny Hanivers*, many specimens lasting for six hundred years or more, but their name remains a mystery. The surname may be a corruption of Antwerp, a bustling seaport of the time, but it is just as possible that some anonymous sailor bestowed the name of his sweetheart or another real woman on the lifelike mummies.

Jerry-built

Here is another of those words for which scholars have offered myriad explanations backed by little proof. Starting with the most ancient sources first, *jerry-built* has been connected with the crumbling walls of *Jericho;* with the prophet *Jeremiah*, because he foretold decay; with the word *jelly*, symbolizing the instability of such structures; and even with the Gypsy word *gerry* meaning "excrement." The most likely theory suggests a corruption of *jerry-mast* or *jeery-mast*, a name sailors gave midway through the last century to makeshift wooden masts. *Jerry masts*, in turn, derive their name from the French *Jour*, a day, indicating their temporary nature. No one seems to take seriously the claim that a Jerry Brothers construction company in Liverpool, England, inspired the word *jerry-built* with its cheap, flimsy constructions, but the term is first found in a Liverpool newspaper in 1861.

Jibber the Kibber

In the late eighteenth century, *to jibber the kibber* meant to fool seamen and wreck ships "by fixing a candle and lantern round the neck of a horse, one of whose fore feet is tied up, this at night has the appearance of another ship's light, and the deceived ship crashes into rocks or a bar." There seems to be no relation to a ship's *jib* in the phrase. In fact, the most anyone can make of the expression is that the *jibber* in it means to confuse, deriving from the verb *to gibber*, to talk confusedly.

John Dory

The European *John Dory* or *St. Peter's cock (Zeus faber)*, a flat, highly valued food fish, had its religious name long before its humorous one. *John Dory* is most likely a jocular designation for some real or imaginary person, perhaps taken from the name of John Dory, a notorious privateer active in the sixteenth century, and the subject of a popular song of the time. Like the haddock, which also has a dark black spot on each side, the golden-yellow *John Dory* has the reputation of being the fish from which the apostle Peter extracted money. In France, it still bears the name *St. Peter's cock;* its oval spots are said to be the finger marks left when Peter held the fish to take the coin from its mouth. The only reference to the story in the Bible is in Matthew 17:27, when Jesus tells Peter how to raise money for the tax collectors: "Notwithstanding, lest we should offend them, go thou to the sea, and cast an hook, and take up the fish that first cometh up; and when thou hast opened his mouth, thou shalt find a piece of money: . . ."

A Johnny-come-lately
Back in the early 1800s, British sailors called any new or inexperienced hand "Johnny Newcomer." American sailors apparently adopted the expression, changing it to "Johnny Comelately." The first recorded mention of the term—in an 1839 novel set on the high seas—uses it in this form in referring to a young recruit. The expression soon came to describe newcomers in all walks of life, changing a little more to the familiar *Johnny-come-lately.*

Jolly Boat
There is nothing particularly jolly about the *jolly boat*, a small craft usually hoisted at a ship's stern. The name of this little workboat, used mostly in harbors, is simply a misspelling of the Dutch *jolle*, meaning a small yawl.

Jolly Roger
French buccaneers may have flown a flag called the *joli rouge* ("pretty red"), and this term may have been corrupted to "Jolly Roger" by English pirates when they transferred it to their black flag. *Jolly Roger* could, however, derive from the seventeenth-century English word "roger," meaning rogue or devil. Or it may come from the widely used Tamil title Ali Raja, meaning "king of the sea," En-

glish pirates pronouncing "Ali Raja" as "Ally Roger," "Olly Roger" and, finally, "Jolly Roger."

A Jonah

Jonah sailed to Tarshish instead of preaching against the evils of Nineveh as the Lord bade him. But the Lord sent a mighty storm to punish him for fleeing, so "that the ship was like to be broken," the frightened sailors aboard deciding that he was an evil influence, a loser, real bad luck. "And they said . . . Come, and let us cast lots, that we may know for whose cause this evil *is* upon us. So they cast lots, and the lot fell upon Jonah" (Jonah 1:7). After they jettisoned Jonah, calm returned to the seas, but Jonah, of course, was swallowed by a giant fish (possibly a whale) and after three days and nights was "vomited out upon dry land," whereupon he did what he was supposed to do in the first place. A *Jonah* still means a bringer of bad luck who spoils the plans of others. The phrase is so popular that it has even become a verb, as in "Don't *jonah* me!"

Junks and Junk

"Junk" was the best pronunciation eighteenth-century British mariners could make of the rude little Javanese sailing boat called a *djong. Junk*, therefore, became the name for the small boat and possibly the word for the things scattered about any ship that seemed as untidy as the *djongs* appeared, though the origin of *junk* in this last respect is not certain.

Kangaroo, Yucatán

Captain James Cook was probably better at geographical discoveries than linguistic ones. Consider the time the great English voyager asked a native of the Australian Endeavor River tribe for the name of a strange marsupial Cook had spotted. The native answered, "Kangaroo," or "I don't know." Cook assumed that this was what the native called the animal, which is how *kangaroo* (or "I don't know") got in the dictionaries. At least that is the derivation several etymologists suggest, there being no better theory, though the story isn't mentioned in any official accounts of Cook's voyages. Similarly, *Yucatán*, meaning "I don't understand you," is supposed to be the answer the Spanish explorer Francisco Fernández de Córdoba received and recorded as a place name in 1517 when he asked a native the name of the area we know today as *Yucatán*.

Keelboat

"These boats were long and narrow, sharp at bow and stern, and of light draft. They were provided with running boards, extending from bow to stern, on each side of the boat," a writer noted in the *American Pioneer* (1843). *Keelboats*, also called *keels* at the time, were first recorded in the language in 1785 and the word derives from the *kiel boot* (meaning the same thing) of early Dutch settlers. *Keelboatmen* were among the roughest of men on the frontier.

Keelhauling, Keelraking

A present-day *keelhauling* is just a tongue-lashing from a superior, hardly even a punishment compared to the original *keelhauling* used as a discipline for Dutch sailors in the sixteenth century. Erring

Dutch sailors, and later seamen in many other navies, were *keel-hauled* by being tied to the yardarm, weighted down and then hauled by a rope under the vessel from side to side. Sometimes they suffered an even more dreaded punishment, being *keelraked*, or hauled under the ship from stem to stern.

Keel Over, an Even Keel

To keel a boat is to roll her over on her keel; that is, to turn up the keel—the bottom of the boat—or to turn her upside down, wrong side uppermost. This nautical practice and term led to the Americanism *to keel over*, first recorded in 1832, which means to turn a man or beast over on his back, to upset or capsize. The expression *to get things on an even keel*, "to make things move smoothly," dates back to at least the early nineteenth century. It, of course, derives from the nautical term *an even keel*, which one early writer defined

Keelhauling was a common naval punishment up until the late nineteenth century
THE COMPLETE ENCYCLOPEDIA OF ILLUSTRATION

this way: "A ship is said to swim on an even keel when she draws the same quantity of water abaft as forward."

Kelpie
There were some benevolent sea monsters of old. The wives of Scottish fishermen, for instance, believed that a black horse with red eyes called the *kelpie* rose from the sea to warn them of forthcoming disasters at sea. The kelpie would then descend into the deep until it could be of help again. However, another Scottish legend has it that an equine water spirit called the *kelpie* delighted in drowning travelers.

Killer Ship
A *killer ship* is a ship of any size on which "death has been caused by her sea behavior"; for example, if someone falls overboard or to the deck from aloft; if there is a fatal accident aboard of any kind; or if she rams another ship and causes death.

Kilroy Was Here
KILROY WAS HERE reigns supreme as the graffito of graffiti in history. No catch phrase has ever rivaled it since it appeared on walls and every other surface capable of absorbing it during World War II. At first it was presumed that Kilroy was fictional; one graffiti expert even insisted that *Kilroy* represented an Oedipal fantasy, combining "kill" with "roi" (the French word for "king"). But it developed that James J. Kilroy, a politician and an inspector in a Quincy, Massachusetts, shipyard coined the slogan. Mr. Kilroy chalked the words on ships and crates of equipment to indicate that he had inspected them and to keep his crews on their toes. From Quincy the phrase traveled on ships and crates all over the world, copied by GI's wherever it went, and Kilroy, who died in Boston in 1962, at the age of sixty, became the most quoted man since Shakespeare.

The Kiss-My-Arse Latitudes
This is the expression, used mostly in the British merchant marine, for the "home stretch," when a ship is close to port and the crew

cares about nothing but getting ashore and tends to ignore orders—especially if the crew has been paid.

Knocked Galley West
Though it came into American use through Mark Twain, who possibly heard it on the Mississippi, no one has been able to explain why a ship's galley or the compass point west have anything to do with this expression, meaning "to knock into smithereens." Perhaps they don't. The term may be a corruption of the English dialect term *collyweston*, which in turn derived from the town of Colly Weston in Northamptonshire, a town given to excessive violence. Colly Weston itself may have been named for a local, violent troublemaker named Colly Weston.

Knots, Dutchman's Log
Knots are the speed of a ship at sea, each knot equaling a nautical mile (6,076) feet, which is slightly longer than a land-measured mile (5,280 feet). Since six nautical (geographical) miles are about equal to seven statute (land) English miles, a ship making 12 knots an hour is actually traveling fourteen land miles. A ship's speed came to be called *knots* because the log line was marked off by knots and has been used to measure a ship's speed since early times. The "log" used in these measurements was often an elaborate *Dutchman's log* engraved with pictures and numbers for timing.

Know the Ropes
Richard Henry Dana used *to know the ropes* in his *Two Years Before the Mast* (1840), but he put the phrase in quotes, indicating that it was an older expression he'd heard. Although this saying, meaning to be skillful, to know all the details of an operation, was common in British racing circles, there is no evidence to indicate that it had its origins in a jockey's expert handling of a horse's reins or "ropes." It is almost surely of nautical birth, referring, of course, to the complex system of ropes on full-rigged sailing ships that bewildered recruits had to master before they became real seamen. Certainly it has nothing to do with boxing because the first instances of its use predate the use of ropes in prizefighting rings. *To learn the ropes* comes from the same nautical source.

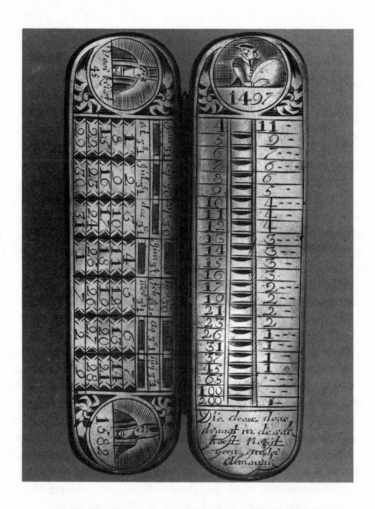

A 1729 Dutchman's log engraved with figures of Julius Caesar and Pope Gregory

110

Lake Hubbs and Company

Marine scientist Dr. Carl L. Hubbs has more marine namesakes than anyone in history. Besides the lake above, twenty-two species of fish, one genus and one species of lichen, one bird, one whale, one crab, two insects, two mollusks, three species of algae, and a research institute are named after this scientist. In addition, a minnow and a lantern fish are named Lauri for his wife.

Landlubber

Lubber meant "a clumsy lout" six centuries ago and this was what sailors originally called green seamen who didn't know a sail from a sheet anchor. Eventually the term was lengthened to *landlubber* and applied to all nonseamen.

Launch

An old word deriving from French, its first recorded nautical use in about 1400 *to launch* did not first mean to break a bottle of champagne against a vessel and slide it into the water. Animal blood was used long before champagne as a sacrifice to the sea gods, red wine later substituted for the blood, and finally more precious champagne substituted for the red wine.

Let the Cat out of the Bag

Some etymologists say that *let the cat out of the bag* originally referred to the master-at-arms aboard a British naval ship taking the cat-o'-nine tails from its blood-red carrying bag before a seaman

111

was flogged. The connection between this and an untimely revelation is a tenuous one, but no better explanation has been offered.

Liberty Ships

Liberty ships were the most common and quickly built ships of all time—built as fast as they were sunk by subs, someone said. During World War II, the *Robert E. Peary*, a *Liberty ship* of prefabricated welded-steel construction weighing 7,200 gross tons, was launched just four days and fifteen and a half hours after the keel laying—the fastest building of a ship ever. She was one of thousands of such transport ships built under the supervision of Henry J. Kaiser (1882–1967) on the Pacific Coast during the war.

Lido

Lido, meaning beach in Italian, was originally the famous resort near Venice, but came to be used generically for any spit of land enclosing a lagoon. The many places throughout the world called Lido Beach literally mean "Beach Beach."

Launching a ship in the early nineteenth century
THE COMPLETE ENCYCLOPEDIA OF ILLUSTRATION

Lightning Never Strikes Twice, St. Barbara

Lightning not only strikes twice in the same place, but is more likely to strike in the same place than not to, simply because the mast, tree or whatever else serving as the conductor for the first strike is the highest, most attractive point in the area. Nevertheless, the old superstition has been around for centuries and is often used in the expression *lightning never strikes twice*, meaning that anything, either bad or good, that happened once won't happen again.

The ancients held that persons struck dead by lightning were incorruptible and honored them. However, many used charms to protect themselves against lightning. The Romans believed that the eagle, the sea calf and laurel warded off lightning, while people in medieval times grew the houseleek *(syngreen)* on ships and on the roofs of their houses to ward it off. Charlemagne ordered all his subjects to do so. Mariners still invoke *St. Barbara* to protect them against lightning. She is the patron saint of those besieged by lightning because a lightning flash killed her unnatural father after he had tortured her and was about to lop off her head with a sword.

The SS Jeremiah O'Brien, *one of the few World War II Liberty ships still surviving, on display at the National Maritime Museum in San Francisco*
RICHARD FREAR, NATIONAL PARK SERVICE PHOTO

113

Lightning, incidentally, kills about 150 people every year in the United States.

Lightning Pilot
A pilot on the Mississippi River in the nineteenth century who was lightning quick, who got all the speed possible from his ship, was called a *lightning pilot.* The term was used by Mark Twain and many other writers.

Lightships, Dumb Ships
Lightships are simply floating lighthouses that warn other ships of danger and serve as aids in navigation, usually in places too distant from shore to erect a permanent structure. Almost all are *dumb ships* unable to navigate themselves, and the first of them seems to have been placed near the River Thames estuary in 1732. The best-known American lightship is probably the Nantucket lightship, which sank in 1935 after the liner *Olympia* rammed it. Today lighted buoys, which provide the same service, are more commonly used than lightships.

Like a Fish out of Water
It is possible that this expression may have originated with the fourth-century Greek patriarch St. Athanasius, but its earliest recorded use is by English theologian John Wyclif in his *English Works* (c. 1380): "And how thei weren out of ther cloistre as fishis withouten water." The metaphor, as widely used as ever today, describes anyone helplessly floundering in an element or environment to which he is unaccustomed.

Like Lemmings
People who follow others blindly, often to their own destruction, are sometimes compared to lemmings, the fabled "rats of Norway" that are supposed to destroy themselves periodically by marching into the sea. Is the lemming's reputation deserved? As Philip Howard wrote in *Verbatim:*

It is probably too late to persuade cartoonists and politicians that no ostrich yet hatched has ever buried its head in the sand. But we ought to try to do something for the unfortunate lemmings. The popular notion that the little rodents commit mass suicide by plunging off the Artic shore and swimming out to a chilly sea is deeply imagined folklore. . . . Like most popular folklore, this is pure nonsense. No credible observer has ever recorded the mass suicide of lemmings. The most that can be said is that on their periodic emigrations to escape from overcrowding, lemmings cross rivers and lakes tumultuously, like migrating ants, and many are drowned. Yet the false idea that

An early lightship battened in a storm

lemmings have a death wish conforms to some evident need in rhetoric . . . evidently we have a need for some vivid metaphor from Nature to illustrate the human propensity to self-destruction.

John Masefield, the great poet of the sea, wrote a touching poem called "Lemmings."

Limey
As far back as 1795, lime juice was issued in the British Navy as an antiscorbutic or protection against scurvy. After about fifty years, Americans and Australians began calling English ships and sailors *lime-juicers*, later *limeys*. The term *limey* was eventually applied to all Englishmen and today the designation and the story behind it is widely known. Originally a contemptuous term, an international slur, *limey* is now rather an affectionate designation.

A Line-of-Battle Ship
In the days of sail, *a line-of-battle ship*, as opposed to other vessels such as frigates, was a capital ship fit to take part in a major battle. "Line of battle" simply meant the formation of ships in a naval engagement.

Littleneck Clams
These tasty clams don't have little necks, but hailed originally from either Little Neck Bay, Long Island, New York, or Little Neck Bay, Ipswich, Massachusetts. No one knows which for sure.

Lloyd's, A-1, Lloyd's Register of Shipping
Lloyd's of London will insure almost anything today, but it began as a maritime insurance group. Lloyd's gives us the expression *A-1*, or *A-One*, for anything excellent, first-class or superior. This was first *A-1 at Lloyd's* and referred to the rating of ships in *Lloyd's Register of Shipping*, the shipping paper published by the insurance association. *A-1* was originally used to denote the highest class of ship and in 1837 Charles Dickens applied the term to people and to things

other than ships. *Lloyd's of London* itself takes its name from a cof-
feehouse operated by one Edward Lloyd, about whom little is known
except that businessmen wanting to insure against sea risks gathered at his place and issued marine policies to shipowners. The association prospered and eventually moved to its present $15 million
palace on Lime Street. Not strictly an insurance company, Lloyd's is
a corporate group of 300 syndicates composed of some 5,500 strictly
supervised individual underwriters, each of whom must deposit
large sums as security against default on the risks each accepts. The
company still boasts that its agents watch every mile of seacoast
throughout the world.

Loaded to the Gills, Loaded to the Guards

Someone *loaded to the gills* "drinks like a fish" (see page 63) or has
drunk alcohol "like a fish drinks water" and is obviously drunk. Sailors use a younger version of the old expression when they say
loaded to the guards. The "guards" here are part of the *Plimsoll lines*
on vessels, marks beyond which it is dangerous to load a ship.

Lobster; Lobster Newburg

Lobsters are, in fact, a kind of bug. The word *lobster* itself is a meld-
ing of two foreign words: the Latin *locasta*, meaning locust, and
the Anglo-Saxon *lappe*, which means spider. "Real" lobster is not
the freshwater lobster that the French call *écrevisse*, or *crawfish*, the
small European crustacean with no claws; or even the warm-water
spiny lobster from which lobster tails are obtained and labeled *lan-
gosta* or *langouste* in some restuarants. The true lobsters number
among their ranks only *Homarus americanus*, often called *Maine* or
North Atlantic lobsters; the smaller *blue lobster* of Europe, *H. vulgaris; Nephrops norvegicus*, the orange *Norwegian lobster*, variously
called *lady lobster, scampi, prawn*, or *crevette rose;* and *H. capensis.*

The most famous of lobster dishes, *Lobster Newburg*, should
have blazoned the name of Benjamin J. Wenberg (1835–1885),
a late-nineteenth-century shipping magnate, across the pages of
menus everywhere, but gastronomical lore has it that he was foolish
enough to displease the great restaurateur Lorenzo Delmonico. It's
said that Wenberg discovered the dish in South America and described it glowingly to Delmonico's owner. Lorenzo, instructing his

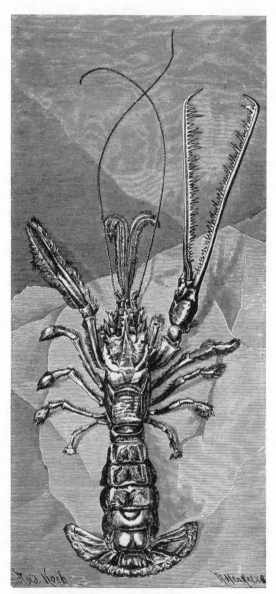

The unusual one-clawed lobster
RICHARD LYDEKKER, THE NEW NATURAL HISTORY, *1895*

chef to prepare the shelled lobster in its rich sauce of sherry, thick cream, and egg yolks, served the dish to his wealthy patron and named it *Lobster Wenberg* in his honor. It remained thus on Delmonico's menu for almost a month, until one evening when Wenberg got drunk, started a fight in the posh restaurant's dining room and was evicted. Soon after, the dish appeared on an enraged Lorenzo's menu as *Lobster Newburg*, probably in honor of the city on the Hudson.

At Loggerheads

Loggerheads are marine turtles found in warm parts of the Atlantic, but the big, knobby-headed turtles have nothing to do with the expression *at loggerheads*—"engaged in a violent quarrel, or a dispute"—even though they are snapping turtles. *At loggerheads* seems to refer to medieval naval battles during which sailors bashed each other with murderous instruments called loggerheads. These loggerheads were long-handled devices with a solid ball of iron on the end that was heated and used to melt pitch or tar, which would be flung at the enemy. The loggerheads themselves apparently made for handy lethal weapons *after* the boiling pitch was used up and mariners from opposing ships probably engaged each other with them, being *at loggerheads*. *Loggerhead* also has an earlier meaning of "an ignorant blockhead, a knucklehead," and this idea of stupidity most likely contributed to the popularity of a phrase that suggests that the people *at loggerheads* in the dispute are headstrong and unwilling to compromise.

Longboat

Longboats were so named because they were the largest boats carried by sailing ships. Up to forty feet long, they had a beam up to eight feet wide and were built to hold great weights.

Longshoreman, Stevedore, Shenango

The *longshoreman*, who helps load and unload ships, gets his name from a contraction of "along-shore-man," while the synonym *stevedore* is from the Spanish *estibador*, "one who packs things." A *shenango* is a specialized longshoreman, one who handles cargo on railroad barges. His name derives from the county Chenango in up-state New York, from where many such workers were once re-cruited.

Look One Way and Row Another
Look one way and row another means to be aimed at one thing, but in reality to be seeking something quite different, like an oarsman rowing a boat. John Bunyan used the expression in *Pilgrim's Progress*.

Loose Lips Sink Ships
During World War II, poster slogans urged sailors and others not to talk about war-related matters, for "The slip of a lip may sink a ship," "Slipped lips sink ships," and "Idle gossip sinks ships." The most memorable of such slogans was *loose lips sink ships*, although a chewing-gum company had great success with "Don't talk, chum, chew Topps gum."

Lorelei
Rising 433 feet high on the right bank of the Rhine River near St. Goar, the *Lorelei* is a rock cliff noted for its strange echo. Centuries ago the legend grew that the steep cliff was the home of a young maiden who had leaped into the Rhine and drowned in dispair over a faithless lover. She was transformed into a siren whose song lured sailors to death in the dangerous Rhine narrows. Those who saw her lost their sight or reason, and those who heard her were condemned to wander with her forever.

Lower the Boom
Lower the boom can mean to hit someone hard, as in *"Clancy lowered the boom."* It can also mean to ask someone for a loan. As a nautical expression the words mean to secure a freighter's cargo booms before she puts out to sea; that is, lower them so that they rest in a cradle parallel to the ship's deck.

LSD, LCI, LCT

These are acronyms for World War II landing ships. The *LSD* (*L*anding *S*hip *D*eck) was a large ship that carried the smaller landing craft which took men and equipment to the beach during amphibious landings. The smaller troop carriers stored in the *LSD's* large inner compartment, which was flooded to launch them, were called *LCIs* (*L*anding *C*raft *I*nfantry), and *LCTs* (*L*anding *C*raft *T*ank) were used for landing tanks.

Lucky Horseshoe

Despite Lord Nelson's belief in them, lucky horseshoes don't have their origin in the sea, as one writer has conjectured. Legend has it that St. Dunstan, a blacksmith who later became Archbishop of Canterbury, outwitted the devil when he asked St. Dunstan to shoe his cloven foot. Recognizing Satan, St. Dunstan tied him up and subjected him to great pain while he shoed him, making the devil promise before he released him that he would never enter a place where a horseshoe was nailed above the door. Another explanation for the lucky horseshoe, put forth by two respected scholars, is that it was originally a symbol of fertility because it roughly resembled the vulva. In any case, Britain's naval hero Lord Nelson believed in the lucky horseshoe and had one nailed to the mast of his flagship *Victory*. He lost his life beneath it at Trafalgar.

Lusitania

Named for the Roman province of Spain, the British liner *Lusitania* is one of the most famous ships in history because her sinking by a German sub started America in the direction of entering World War I against Germany. Many Americans were among the 1,195 people on the *Lusitania* when she went down off Old Head of Kinsale in 1915. Most historians believe the tragedy was the fault of both a brutal submarine commander and the pig-headed skipper of the *Lusitania*, who refused to stay away from dangerous waters or even to speed through them.

Mae West

It's probably an apocryphal tale, but "Come up and see me some-time!" is what the soldier, sailor or airman who invented the term *Mae West* is supposed to have said when he tried on his lifejacket and noticed that he bulged prominently where the famous movie queen did. We do know that the inflatable life jacket was introduced at the beginning of World War II and named for one of the most famous sex symbols because it "bulged in the right places." Mae West (1893–1980) starred on Broadway until two of her plays, *Sex* and *Pleasure Man*, were closed by the police in 1928. Migrating to Hollywood, she won fame as "Diamond Lil," the "Screen's Bad Girl," and the "Siren of the Screen." Her name, *Webster*'s advises, is also given to a *twin-turreted* tank, a malfunctioning parachute with a *two-lobed* appearance, and a *bulging* sail.

The Maelstrom, or Malstrom

The best-known whirlpool in the world is the Malstrom, found in the waters of the Lofoten Islands off Norway's west coast. Norwegians also call it the Moskenstrom or Moskenstraumen. *Maelstrom* is a Norwegian word deriving from the Dutch *malen* ("to grind or whirl"), and *strom* ("stream")—hence "grinding stream." One leg-end surrounding the maelstrom has it that two magic millstones aboard a vessel sailing this passage ground out so much salt that the ship foundered, but the millstones still continued to grind away un-derwater, making the surrounding waters "forever turbulent and salty." *Maelstrom* was first used to describe this Norwegian phenom-enon alone, but has since come to mean all large whirlpools the world over and widespread turmoil in general.

Making Both Ends Meet

There have been some fanciful speculations that the expression *to make both ends meet* derives from the practice of splicing rope together on old sailing ships to save money. The phrase, however, seems to be merely a shortening of *to make both ends of the year meet*, meaning the same—to live within one's income. Tobias Smollett first recorded the saying in his picturesque novel *The Adventures of Roderick Random* (1748).

Malakoff

Malakoff, or Malakhov, a fortified hill overlooking Sevastopol from the east, was the scene of one of the most publicized battles of the Crimean War. After a long siege, the French finally stormed Malakoff and took it on September 8, 1855. The historic hill is supposed to be named for a drunken Russian sailor who set up a liquor store on the heights after being fired from his job in the Sevastopol shipyards. Houses and finally fortifications were built around him and he ultimately won more fame than most of his more sober contemporaries. At one time a crinoline also honored the man's name and today the reformed drunkard is remembered for *malakoff*, a restricted form of four-handed dominoes, and *malakoff*, a small French cream cheese, which both commemorate the battle fought on his famous hill.

A Man Doesn't Get His Hands out of the Tar by Becoming Second Mate

This saying is from the age of sail, when only the *first* mate was exempted from the dirty work of sticking his hands into the tar bucket for tarring the rigging. It is used colloquially to indicate that responsibilities don't end with promotion.

Man or Girl Friday

Daniel Defoe's *Robinson Crusoe* gives us the term *man Friday* or *girl Friday*, a hardworking helper or servant, who is knowledgeable of all aspects of a business. The prototype was of course the castaway's native companion Friday.

Marble Boat, Concrete Boat

Legend says that the relics of the apostle St. James were miraculously transported from Jerusalem in a marble boat with sails, and a huge stone used to be exhibited as this boat at Padrón on the Spanish coast. It is definitely no legend that concrete boats were built in the United States during World War I to help conserve steel. These reinforced concrete ships performed well but weren't kept in operation after the war.

Marina

Shortly after World War II, Americans began employing the term *marina* for a modern harbor or boat basin used exclusively or primarily for private yachts and speedboats. Today thousands of *marinas* serve boat owners. Some are small harbors mooring fifty boats, while others hold one hundred times that many. The largest marina in the world is Marina del Rey in Los Angeles, California, with berths for seventy-five hundred yachts.

Mark Twain!

It is well known that former riverboat pilot Samuel Langhorne Clemens took his pen name Mark Twain from the leadsman's call *Mark twain!* ("mark two fathoms"). *Mark twain!* itself is a slurred mispronunciation of "Mark on the twine, six fathoms!," called out when riverboat leadsmen sounded the river with weighted twine.

Martha's Vineyard

Believed to have been discovered by Leif Ericson in the eleventh century, *Martha's Vineyard*, an island about five miles off Massachusetts's southeast coast, was once an important center for whaling and fishing. The Indians called the island *Noe-pe*, "Amid the Waters," while the Norsemen named it Straumey, "Isle of Currents." It was christened *Martin's Vineyard* by English navigator Bartholomew Gosnold in 1602 for no known reason. After a century it took the name *Martha's Vineyard*, probably because its name was confused with that of a little neighboring island to the southwest called Martha's Vineyard that had also been named by Gosnold. That little island is now called *No Mans Land*, after an Indian named Teque-noman. (See also *Nantucket*, page 133.)

Mayflower, *the* Mayflower *Compact*
The *Mayflower*, the former wine ship that transported the founding fathers to America, took its name from the mayflower, another name for the blossom of the hawthorn tree. In the *Mayflower Compact*, signed by the fifty-one adult passengers aboard ship, all agreed to stay together where they landed, choose their own leader and abide by majority rule. This was the rude beginning of American democracy.

Mayonnaise
Portus Magonis in Minorca was named after Hannibal's brother, Mago, sometime in the early second century. Eventually the capital of the Mediterranean Balearic island become known as *Port Mahon* or *Mahón* and Port Mahon gave its name to *mayonnaise*. The story is that the Duc de Richelieu attacked the island and drove out the British for a while in 1756. But Richelieu—noted for his love of delicious food and delectable women, as exemplified by his naked dinner parties back in France—was ravenously hungry after the battle. The Frenchman stormed the nearest kitchen ashore, tossed all the food he could find into one pot and blended it all together. This possibly apocryphal tale got back to Paris, where chefs concocted a dressing of blended-together ingredients that they named *Mahonnaise* in honor of Richelieu's victory at Port Mahon.

Mediterranean Sea
Deriving from the Latin *medi*, "middle," and *terraneus*, "earth," the *Mediterranean* means "the sea in the middle of the earth," which, indeed, the ancients believed it to be.

Mermaid
Mermaids, whose name derives from the Latin *mer* ("sea"), date back long before written history. In Greek mythology the fifty daughters of Nereus, the god of the sea, were beautiful mermaids who rode

the waves on the backs of dolphins, and any sailor lucky enough to catch one could demand that the mermaid predict the future as a price for letting her go. Mermaid tales are part of the folklore of every country on or near the sea. There are legends of mermaids who foretell the future; of mermaids who give "wishes three" to anyone who catches them; and of mermaids who protect a favored sailor and punish anyone who harms him. Popular, too, are yarns about mermaids who fall in love with sailors; the mermaid who lives with a man as his lawful wife and, after being betrayed by him in some way, causes a disaster and sorrowfully swims away; or the mermaid who falls in love with a lusty mariner and entices him to reside with her down in Davy Jones's Locker (see page 57). There

Manatees like this one, and dugongs standing erect with their young in their armlike flippers, were often mistaken for mermaids by lonely sailors

MARINELAND OF FLORIDA

has always been poetic license with mermaids, but the creatures do have some basis in reality. Many scientists believe that they are based on sailors' accounts of a living creature called the *dugong*, a large, white marine mammal that often stands upright in the water cradling its young in flippers that from a distance look like arms.

Mermaid's Purses, Mermaid's Glove

The horny skate, ray and shark-egg cases often washed up on the beach by wave action are popularly called *mermaid's purses*. A *mermaid's glove* is a British sponge (*Halichondria palmata*) whose branches resemble human fingers.

A Message to Garcia

Elbert Hubbard's inspirational essay *A Message to Garcia*, first published in his magazine *The Philistine* in 1899, remained required reading in most elementary-school English classes until about twenty-five years ago. Hubbard's essay dramatized the true adventure of Lieutenant Andrew Summers Rowan, U.S. Bureau of Naval Intelligence, who during the Spanish-American War was sent by the U.S. Chief of Staff to communicate with General Calixto García, leader of the Cuban insurgent forces. No one knew just where the elusive García might be, but Rowan made his way through the Spanish blockade in a small boat, landing near Turquino Peak on April 24, 1898, where he contacted local patriots who directed him to García far inland and returned to Washington with information regarding the insurgent forces. The brave and resourceful Rowan became a hero, but Hubbard transformed him into an almost Arthurian figure and it was his essay that made *carry a message to Garcia* a byword. Hubbard, who went down with the *Lusitania*, also wrote an *Essay on Silence*. Published in 1898 it contained nothing but blank pages.

Mickey Mouse Rules

One theory holds that World War II U.S. Navy Military Indoctrination Centers, or M.I.C.s, where undisciplined sailors were restrained, gave their initials to this expression for petty rules. The expression has been around since early in World War II and probably can be explained by the fact that such rules seem silly and childish, like

Mickey Mouse cartoons. Mickey Mouse was better honored when his name became the password chosen by intelligence officers in planning the greatest invasion in the history of warfare—Normandy, 1944. *Mickey Mouse diagrams* were maps made for plotting positions of convoys and bombarding forces at Normandy.

The Middle Passage, Triangular Trade
In the so-called *triangular trade*, ships carried New England rum to the African Gold Coast on the first passage, traded the rum for slaves and transported the shackled slaves to the West Indies on *the middle passage*, where the slaves were sold for molasses and sugar, which were brought back to New England to make more rum on the final passage. The *middle passage* was, of course, the worst and most inhuman of the three legs of the journey.

Midshipman Fish, "Talking Fish"
Common to mainland America, the midshipman fish (*Porichthys notatus*) has golden spots on each side like the brass buttons on a midshipman's coat. Familiar along the Pacific coast, the luminescent midshipman is also called "the talking fish," the "grunter," the "grunt" and the "singing fish." The sound it makes when disturbed—made by vibrating its air bladder—is actually similar to the croak of a tree frog. Other "talking fish" include the triggerfish, which is called *Humuhumunkunukn-a-puaa*, "fish that grunts like a pig," by Hawaiians, and the male codfish, which grunts, both to defend its spawning area and to urge females to lay eggs. A Gulf of Mexico toadfish species has an air bladder that actually produces "a powerful hooting sound . . . resembling a boat whistle," according to one marine biologist.

Mind Your P's and Q's
Citing deficiencies in other theories, several etymologists suggest a nautical derivation here. Solicitous wives, they claim, told their seamen husbands to mind their *p*'s and *q*'s, not to let their *pea* jackets be soiled by their greasy, often tarred, *queues* (pigtails)! More likely the expression has something to do with schoolchildren being told to mind their *p*'s and *q*'s when learning the alphabet.

Moby-Dick

Mocha Dick, "the stout gentleman of the latitudes, the prodigious terror whale of the Pacific, the redoubtable white sperm whale that fought and won a hundred sea battles against overwhelming odds" —such was the reputation in the extravagant language of the time of the whale Herman Melville immortalized as *Moby-Dick*. There is no doubt about it: Mocha Dick was a real whale. Dick was probably first fought in 1819, the year Melville was born, and he was still terrorizing whalemen when the author was writing *Moby-Dick* in 1850.

Melville probably first read about Mocha Dick in a piece by Jeremiah N. Reynolds in the May 1839 *Knickerbocker Magazine*. Reynolds told how Dick was sighted and fought off the coast of Chile near the conical peak of Mocha Island, from which the white whale took his name. Undoubtedly, though, he had heard of him before in the fo'c'sles of the ships he sailed. The last mention in history of

The whaling print "Pêche du Cachelot," praised by Herman Melville in Moby-Dick *for its accuracy, can be seen in the Colchester lighthouse marine gallery*
SHELBURNE MUSEUM, SHELBURNE, VERMONT

Mocha Dick is dated August 1859, when, off the Brazilian banks, he is said to have been taken by a Swedish whaler. Measuring 110 feet in length, he weighed more than a ton for each foot. The whale that Melville and others believed caused the 1819 *Essex* sinking, which formed the basis for *Moby-Dick*, was captured without much of a struggle. The Swedish whaler's log discloses he was dying of old age, blind in his right eye, his head a mass of scars, eight teeth broken off and the others all worn down.

But no one would ever remember him this way. He had already become legend when Herman Melville wrote *Moby-Dick*. Melville changed his first name to *Moby*, probably to suggest his amazing *mobi*lity and to avoid association with the "color" mocha. Melville had made Dick something more than a whale. Mocha Dick, in the words of one writer, "had been absolved of mortality. . . . Readers of *Moby-Dick* know that he swims the world unconquered, that he is ubiquitous in time and place."

Molly

Few home aquarium owners know that this popular tropical fish takes its feminine name from a man. French Count François Nicolas Mollien (1758–1850) wasn't a tropical-fish collector—the hobby only dates back to about 1860—but a French financial genius who served Napoleon, though the emperor stubbornly refused to accept his good advice. Mollien nevertheless won fame and the tropical freshwater fish genus *Mollienesia* was named in his honor; all *mollies* bear his abbreviated surname.

The Monitor *and the* Merrimack

Though the Civil War battle of the *Monitor* and the *Merrimack*, the first ironclad action at sea, is a familiar one, there is usually some confusion about the names of the southern vessel involved. Actually, she was launched as the *Merrimack* in 1855 at the Boston Navy Yard and was originally a wooden steam frigate. She was then seized by the Confederacy in 1861, encased in dry dock with double layers of railroad iron and renamed the *Virginia* and then launched in 1862. After that time she was called both the *Merrimack* and the *Virginia*, even though only the last name was correct. In fact, she was most often referred to as the *Merrimac* (without the terminal *k*) over the years, a spelling that is totally unjustified.

Moon Cussers

Moon cussers cussed the moon and the light that it brought because it robbed them of their livelihood. During the early nineteenth century, these lowlifes lured merchant ships to shore on dark nights by waving lanterns that were mistaken for the lights of other vessels. When the ships were destroyed on the rocks, their cargo was collected as salvage.

A Murmansk Run

A Murmansk run became the synonym for a dangerous sea voyage during World War II, when hundreds of cargo ships were sunk by Nazi subs and planes while on course across the North Atlantic to the ice-free Russian port of Murmansk.

The Monitor *attacking the* Merrimack

Mussel

Oddly enough, *mussels* take their name from the common house mouse. Both the muscles in our bodies and the mussels in the sea share this derivation and we owe it to the early Romans, who had a sense of humor as well as lusty appetites. The Romans rather whimsically thought that body muscles, appearing and disappearing as men competed in athletic games and then rested, resembled tiny mice appearing and disappearing at play. Similarly, little dark-colored mice were also thought to resemble the dark-colored marine bivalves the Romans liked to serve at their banquets. Thus, both the muscle and the mussel were named *musculus*, or "little mouse." The marine mussel's name is spelled differently today only because this makes it easier to distinguish it from "muscle."

The Naked Truth

When Truth went swimming in the river, Falsehood stole Truth's clothes, according to an ancient Roman fable, and Truth went naked rather than put on Falsehood's clothes. Such is the origin of *nuda veritas* or the *naked truth*, which can be traced back as far as the writings of Horace.

The Names of Young Water Creatures

Beaver: kit
Birds: fledgling, nestling
Codfish: codling, sprag
Eel: elver
Fish (generally): fry
Frog: polliwog, tadpole
Mackerel: blinker, tinker, spike
Salmon: parr, smolt, grilse
Seal: pup
Sea Lion: pup
Shark: cub
Swan: cygnet
Whale: calf

Nantucket

There is a hoary tale, probably untrue, that an old seaman owned the island groups off Massachusetts. To his favorite daughter he gave his most productive island, Martha's Vineyard; to his next, he gave the islands closest to home, Elizabeth's Island; and to his last ·

daughter, Nan, he just offered what remained, and *Nan-tuck-it.* (See also Martha's Vineyard, page 124).

Narwhal
The narwhal of arctic waters, a whale that grows up to twenty feet long and has an eight-foot-long tusk, takes its name from the Scandinavian *nar*, "ghost" or "corpse" (for its white color) and the Scandinavian word for whale. The narwhal is probably responsible for the legend of the unicorn so widely believed in medieval times. This "unicorn of the sea" uses its long tusk, or left incisor tooth, which grows outward in a counterclockwise spiral, to battle other narwhals. Only the male of the species has the tusk, employing it during the mating season when fighting over females.

A common method of hunting narwhals in the nineteenth century
MAMMALIA: THEIR VARIOUS FORMS AND HABITS, *1890*

The Naumachia, where the Romans held sea battles on land

The Complete Encyclopedia of Illustration

The Naumachia

Roman emperors held "sea battles" on land in the *Naumachia*, a flooded amphitheater Augustus built on the right back of the Tiber River. The combatants in the two opposing fleets, who were usually prisoners or criminals, fought to the death unless spared by the emperor. As many as twenty-four triremes fought in these bloody contests.

Naval War Slogans

An informal survey suggests that the seven sayings recorded below are the best known of naval war slogans:

> "I have not yet begun to fight!" —John Paul Jones, Revolutionary War
> "We have met the enemy and they are ours." —Oliver H. Perry, War of 1812.
> "Don't give up the ship!" —John Lawrence, War of 1812. (He

may really have said, "Tell the men to fire faster and not to give up the ship until she sinks.")

"Damn the torpedoes! Full speed ahead!" —David Farragut, Civil War

"Remember the Maine!" —Anonymous slogan, Spanish-American War

"You may fire when you are ready, Gridley." —George Dewey, Spanish-American War

"Remember Pearl Harbor!" —Anonymous slogan, World War II

Navy Blue, Navy

Navy blue made its debut in the Royal Navy in 1857, when for the first time an act of Parliament required English sailors to wear identical uniforms. This outfit included a blue jacket, which inspired the name of the color *navy blue* or *navy* shortly after it became standard issue. Today any *navy blue* clothing takes its name from the color of that first *navy blue* jacket.

"Nearer, My God, to Thee"

Legend has it that the famous White Star liner *Titanic* went down while the ship's orchestra played the hymn "Nearer, My God, to Thee." This is a charming story that has been repeated in numerous accounts of the *Titanic* sinking, but actually, the orchestra had been playing ragtime as the end approached. Their last number was the Anglican hymn "Autumn."

Nelson's Blood

Lord Horatio Nelson, Britain's greatest naval hero, was killed at the battle of Trafalgar in 1805 by a sniper firing from the top of the French ship *Redoubtable*, and his body was brought back to England to be buried in St. Paul's Cathedral. The fabled hero, who had lost an eye in one sea battle and an arm in another, became the subject of many legends, including one that his body was brought home pickled in rum. Needless to say, it wasn't long before British sailors were calling rum *Nelson's blood.*

Neptune, Poseidon and Company

Neptune, the Roman god of the water, is usually represented as a stately old man carrying a trident and sitting astride a dolphin or huge sea horse called a *Hippocampus.* The ruler or king of the sea, his name is used for the sea itself. *Poseidon* was the god of the sea in Greek mythology, his wife, *Amphitrite*, the goddess of the sea. Other sea gods include *Triton*, their son; *Nereus*, his hair seaweed green, who lives with his wife *Doris* at the bottom of the Mediterranean; *Portunus*, the protector of harbors; and *Oceanus*, god of the ocean. There were also fifty *nereids*, daughters of Nereus, and the *oceanids*, daughters of Oceanus.

The Ninth Wave

> And then the two
> Dropt to the cove, and watch'd the great sea fall,
> Wave after wave, each mightier than the last,
> Till last, a ninth one, gathering half the deep
> And full of voices, slowly rose and plunged
> Roaring, and all the wave was in a flame.
> —ALFRED, LORD TENNYSON, "The Holy Grail"

An old nautical superstition holds that waves become progressively higher until the ninth wave (some say the tenth) and that then the progression begins all over again. While waves sometimes form larger ones when they meet, there is no fixed interval when a large one can be predicted.

No Room to Swing a Cat

One plausible explanation for this expression points to a sailor's hammock or "cat" and there being little room on ships of old to swing one. But there are no quotations to support this theory and the derivation must be marked "uncertain."

Noah's Ark

It is safe to say that everyone over the age of six is familiar with the biblical story of Noah's Ark. But few are aware of this entry in the New York files of the Atlantic Mutual Insurance Company, which has one of the largest archives on marine disasters in the world:

> Noah's Ark. Built in 2448 B.C. Gopher wood, pitched within and without. Length, three hundred cubits; width, 50 cubits; height, 30 cubits. Three decks. Cattle carrier. Owner: Noah and Sons. Last reported stranded Mount Ararat.

Noah's Brig

A tiny rockbound island in the Hudson River, *Noah's Brig* is named for one Captain Noah, an old-time captain of a fleet of rafts who had the misfortune of encountering the island under adverse conditions one night. Noah sighted "a dark object floating the waters" that looked like a brig under sail. "Brig ahoy!" he cried, but no answer came. "Brig ahoy!" he shouted. "Answer or I'll run you down!" There was still no reply and Captain Noah stubbornly held his course. Then a crash—wood crunched rock: Noah had mistaken two trees on the island for masts with sails set.

A Nosey Parker

Many candidates have been proposed as the original *Nosey Parker*, which means a busybody or unduly inquisitive person. Richard Parker, leader of the Sheerness mutiny in 1797, is a strong contender. This Parker poked his nose so deeply into what the military thought its exclusive bailiwick that he wound up hanged from the yardarm of H.M.S. *Sandwich*. Then there were the Duke of Wellington and Oliver Cromwell, both known as "Nosey" because of their prominent noses.

But the leading contender is Matthew Parker, who became Archbishop of Canterbury in 1559, and had acquired a reputation for poking his nose into other people's business. Actually, he was an intelligent, if somewhat overzealous, churchman of marked Protestant persuasion who introduced many administrative and ceremonial reforms into the Anglican Church. His reputation is largely undeserved, but Catholics and Puritans alike resented his good works, taking advantage of his rather long nose and dubbing him *Nosey Parker* is first recorded in 1908 and makes no reference to any of the gentlemen above. If the archbishop or one of the others is the original *Nosey Parker*, somebody probably borrowed his name for the term centuries later.

Oakum

Sailors and prisoners were once forced to unravel old tarred rope and unpick its fiber with their bare hands, a job that could rip the flesh to shreds after a short time. The fiber was called *oakum*, which was used to caulk the seams in the timbers of wooden ships.

O'Donohue's White Horses

Every seven years on May Day, the Irish chieftain O'Donohue returns to the Lakes of Killarney riding his great white steed, gliding over the waters to sweet but unearthly music, a host of fairies preceding him and strewing his path with spring flowers. Foaming waves on a windy day are thus known as *O'Donohue's white horses*. Legend has it that more than one beautiful young girl believed in O'Donohue so strongly that she threw herself into the water so that he would carry her off for his bride.

O-grab-me

President James Madison's Embargo Act of 1807, and acts of following years, restricted American ship departures to prevent hostilities on the seas. But since it hurt our British and French enemies less than American shipowners (the policy having the reverse effect of the one intended), shipowners began spelling *embargo* backward and called the acts the "o-grab-me acts." Wrote one shipping magnate to another: "As soon as O'grab-me! shall go his end, I'll haste to relate the sweet tidings to you."

Old Glory

America's flag was not named *Old Glory* by Betsy Ross during the Revolutionary War. In fact, the many paintings that show the Stars and Stripes flying at Valley Forge and in major battles of the Revolution are all in error, for no official stars-and-strips flags were used by the Army until 1783. Old Glory was named by Captain William Driver of the brig *Charles Doggett* on August 10, 1831. Captain Driver had brought back the British mutineers of the H.M.S. *Bounty* from Tahiti to their home on Pitcairn Island, and some say that in recognition of this humane service a band of women presented him with a large American flag. Others claim that friends gave him the flag as a present. In any case, as he hoisted the flag to the masthead, he proclaimed, "I name thee Old Glory." His ship's flag became famous and by 1850 its name became common for the flag in general. The original Old Glory is now on display in the Smithsonian Institution in Washington, D.C.

Old Ironsides, *the* Constitution

The *Constitution*, built six months after the *Constellation* (see page 51), is America's oldest warship still afloat and in commission. A national historic monument today, she is moored in Boston Harbor flying the flag of the commandant of the First Naval District. The high point of her illustrious career came on August 19, 1812, when she engaged and defeated the British frigate *Guerrière* off Nova Scotia. During the battle an American sailor, watching British shots fall into the sea, cried: "Huzza! Her sides are made of iron!" and *Old Ironsides* she has been since that day. In 1830 Oliver Wendell Holmes, hearing that she was to be sold by the Navy, wrote his poem "Old Ironsides" in protest and she was saved.

> Ay tear her tattered ensign down!
>   Long has it waved on high,
> And many an eye has danced to see
>   That banner in the sky,
> Beneath it rung the battle shout,
>   And burst the cannon's roar;
> The meteor of the ocean air
>   Shall sweep the clouds no more.

Her decks, once red with heroes' blood,
  Where knelt the vanquished foe,
When winds were carrying o'er the flood
  And waves were white below,
No more shall feel the victor's tread,
  Or know the conquered knee;
The harpies of the shore shall pluck
  The eagle of the sea!

Historic Old Ironsides *can still be visited at the Charlestown Navy Yard in Boston*
THE COMPLETE ENCYCLOPEDIA OF ILLUSTRATION

Oh better that her shattered hulk
  Should sink beneath the wave
Her thunders shook the mighty deep
  And there should be her grave;
Nail to the mast her holy flag,
  Set every threadbare sail,
And give her to the god of storms,
  The lightning and the gale!

Old Whale, Sardine

By now obsolete, these all but forgotten terms were colorful expressions for sailors in the early nineteenth century. Wrote one old salt in a New Haven newspaper in 1861: "We 'Old Whales' or, as we are sometimes termed, 'Sardines,' are not supposed by some 'land crabs' [landlubbers] to have much of a taste for the feathery tribe [chicken] 'done up brown.'"

On the Rocks

Here the allusion is to a ship grounded off a rocky coast, battered by waves and ready to sink, and the expression arose among seamen, as would be expected. The figurative use of rocks for a symbol of destruction or ruin dates back to at least the early sixteenth century, but it wasn't until three hundred years later (1889) that the phrase *on the rocks* appeared or is first recorded. When we use the expression today we always refer to ruin or impending disaster. Someone *on the rocks* can be stone broke, or bereft of sanity. A marriage *on the rocks* is wrecked and about to be sunk unless it is saved at the last minute. Even a drink *on the rocks* (liquor or wine served over ice cubes, which resemble rocks) might be said to be the cause of someone going under.

On Your Own Hook

New England fishermen on boats fishing the Grand Banks in days past were paid according to what they caught individually on their own hooks and lines. To this practice we owe the expression *to be on your own hook*, to be on your own.

Ostracism

How did the word *ostracism*, to banish socially in some way, come from *ostrakon*, the Greek word for oyster shell? It seems that a vote of banishment in ancient Athens had to be a written one, for it was, of course, a serious matter to send a person into exile for crimes against the state. Since paper or papyrus was scarce, the banishment ballot was written on pieces of tile called *ostrakon*, this name having first been applied to the shell of the oyster, which the tile resembled. It followed that the name *ostrakismos* be bestowed upon the act of banishment itself, which gives us our word for "to banish socially"—to *ostracize* or "oyster shell."

(To Have Someone) Over a Barrel

The sense of this Americanism is that the person over the barrel is in the other person's powers or at his mercy. In the days before mouth-to-mouth resuscitation and other modern methods of life-saving, lifeguards placed drowning victims over a barrel, which was rolled back and forth while the lifeguard tried to revive them. Victims were certainly in the lifeguard's power and the process is probably the origin of the phrase.

Overwhelm

Whelm and *overwhelm* mean essentially the same thing, to be completely overcome by something, but *overwhelm* is a stronger, more emphatic term. In any case, *whelm*, the source of *overwhelm*, is a sea word, having its roots in the Middle English *whelven*, meaning to capsize or turn a vessel upside down. The English *whelm* was first recorded in the thirteenth century and soon took on the sense of turning a vessel upside down "so as to cover it" with water, which led to its modern meaning.

Oysters Kirkpatrick

Oysters Rockefeller's closest rival was named in honor of James C. Kirkpatrick, manager of San Francisco's Palace Hotel in the late nineteenth century. *Oysters Kirkpatrick* shares its fame with Green Goddess dressing and Strawberries Romanoff, also invented in the Palace's kitchen. The Palace Hotel, born during the Gold Rush of

1849, destroyed in the earthquake of 1900 and rebuilt to become one of America's greatest eating places, offers the following simple original recipe for the delectable dish: "Open oysters on deep shell, put in oven for about 3 or 4 minutes until oysters shrink. Pour off the liquor, then add small strip of bacon and cover with catsup and place in very hot oven for about 5 or 6 minutes until glazed to a nice golden brown."

Oysters Rockefeller

Oysters Rockefeller, bivalves broiled with a puree of spinach, other vegetables and seasonings on a bed of rock salt, probably originated in 1899 at Antoine's, the famous New Orleans restaurant. The first customer to taste the fabulous dish is supposed to have said, "It's as rich as Rockefeller," the name appearing on the menu shortly afterward.

Pacific Ocean

The courageous Portuguese explorer Ferdinand Magellan gave this great ocean its name in 1520, because of the calm, peaceful weather he enjoyed on it after a stormy passage in adjoining straits. It might, therefore, be said that he named the biggest thing on earth.

Paddle Your Own Canoe

Abraham Lincoln's frequent use of this phrase did much to make it popular, but Captain Frederick Marryat, that unflattering critic of American manners, seems first to have used the words in their figurative sense, "be independent," in his novel *The Settlers in Canada* (1844): "I think it much better that . . . every man paddle his own canoe." More currency was given the saying with the publication in *Harper's Monthly* (May 1854) of a song by Dr. Edward P. Philpots, the refrain of which went:

> *Voyager upon life's sea:*
> *To yourself be true,*
> *And what'er your lot may be,*
> *Paddle your own canoe.*

Canoe probably derives from the Arawak word *canoa*, for a small boat carved from a tree trunk, which Columbus recorded in his diary and introduced into Spanish.

Passion Killers

During World War II, the Wrens (Women's Royal Navy Service) were issued long, plain, unstylish black knickers or underwear that they or other interested parties promptly dubbed *passion killers*, at least getting even with the powers-that-were by way of the King's English.

The Paul Jones Dance

"Sir, I have not yet begun to fight" is the reply traditionally ascribed to John Paul Jones when British Captain Richard Pearson of the *Serapis* demanded that he surrender the sinking *Bonhomme Richard*. Jones won the celebrated Revolutionary War sea battle off Scarborough, England, boarding the *Serapis* after a three-and-a-half-hour struggle by moonlight. The casualties were so great on each side that neither captain ever issued a complete casualty list. The intrepid seaman came to be regarded as America's greatest naval hero and founder of the American naval tradition, but his genius wasn't much appreciated in his own time.

The naval hero's real name was John Paul, not John Paul Jones. Born near Kirkcudbright, Scotland, John Paul went to sea when only twelve, serving as first mate aboard a slaver and even having some experience ashore as an actor before receiving his first command in 1770. It was then that his troubles began. A ship's carpenter he had had flogged for laziness died, resulting in a murder charge. Released on bail, John Paul purchased a ship in the West Indies in order to hunt for evidence proving his innocence. But in 1773 he killed the ringleader of a mutinous crew, and to avoid trial again he fled to America, changed his name to John Paul Jones and received a commission as a lieutenant in the new Continental navy under this name in 1775. His naval genius soon resulted in a promotion to captain and command of the *Ranger*, whose daring raids off England were climaxed with the capture of the British warship *Drake*, the first ever to surrender to an American vessel. But political machinations, which plagued him and obscured his fame all his life, forced Jones to relinquish command of *Ranger*. It was on the old rebuilt merchantman named *Bonhomme Richard*, in honor of Benjamin Franklin and his *Poor Richard's Almanac*, that he fought his most famous battle. It is little known that Jones became a rear admiral in the Russian navy after the Revolutionary War. Here again political intrigue and scandal prevented his recognition: His victories against the Turks were credited to others and his name was dishonored when he was falsely accused of a criminal assault on a young girl.

John Paul Jones died a broken and embittered man in Paris in

1792 when only forty-five. Buried in an unmarked grave in the St. Louis Cemetery for Protestants, it was more than a century before his remains were brought back to America to be enshrined in a crypt in the naval chapel at Annapolis. Jones had greatly enjoyed dancing in his youth. The Paul Jones dance, a popular square dance featuring promenades and numerous changes of partners, was named for him during the Revolution, one of the few honors accorded his name at the time.

Pea Jacket

The *pea jacket* was not originally a P-jacket (an abbreviation of *pilot's jacket*), but derives from the Dutch *pijjekker*, a short double-breasted coat very similar to the pea jacket of today that was worn by Dutch sailors as early as the fifteenth century.

The Peacemaker

Swedish engineer John Ericsson was responsible for the first screw-propeller warship, the *Princeton*, which embodied his ideas when built at the Philadelphia Navy Yard in 1843. A year later another of Ericsson's ideas was incorporated in a big gun for the *Princeton*. It was called the *Peacemaker*, and its breech was strengthened with wrought iron. However, the *Peacemaker*, unlike the screw propeller, became one of the most famous guns in U.S. naval history because it was a failure. In February 1844, President John Tyler and some two hundred prominent guests took a cruise down the Potomac aboard the *Princeton* to witness the highly touted gun being tested. When it was fired, the *Peacemaker* exploded in its breech, killing the Secretary of State, the Secretary of the Navy and three others. President Tyler only escaped because he was dining belowdecks with his fiancée.

Pelican

No woodpecker is the *pelican*, but in his famous translation of the Bible, St. Jerome, thinking it pecked wood like a woodpecker, named the bird *pelican*, from the Greek word *pelekys*, or "ax beak." The name stuck, as did many legends about the bird, including one that it resurrected its dead young by feeding them its blood—a myth stemming from the fact that the pelican macerates fish in the large sack under its bill and feeds it to its young. Wrote Dixon Lanier Merrith in his poem "The Pelican" (1910):

> A wonderful bird is the
>   pelican,
> His bill will hold more than his
>   belican.
> He can take in his beak
> Food enough for a week,
> But I'm damned if I see how the
>   helican.

President John Tyler was nearly killed when the celebrated gun Peacemaker *blew up in a demonstration on the* Princeton *in 1893*

Penguin

The penguin looks nothing like one would expect it to, judging by its name. Though the bird has a black head, its name derives from Welsh words meaning "white head": *pen*, "head," and *gwyn*, "white." Welsh sailors were responsible for this odd christening when they gave the name *penguin* to the great auk, a flightless bird with white spots on its head that was common on North Atlantic islands in the sixteenth century. For some reason lost in history, sailors in other oceans later transferred the name *penguin* to the flightless bird so named today.

Peter Boat, Petrels, Mother Carey's Chickens

It is not often that the exact origin of a first name is recorded, especially a common one like Peter, but the fact remains that every Peter ever born derives his given name from St. Peter. Peter was the name Christ gave the "Prince of the Apostles." This was apparently the first time the name was ever used: "That thou art Peter," Christ tells his disciple, "and upon this rock I will build my church; and the gates of hell shall not prevail against it (*Matthew* 16:18)." This is the authority on which the papacy is based, and Christ uses the name Peter just after addressing his disciple by his proper name, Simon Bär-jona: Simon, the son of Jonah. Simon's new name, meaning stone, though translated as rock, is *Cephas* in Aramaic, but *Petros* in Greek and *Petrus* in Latin, both latter words giving us the name *Peter*, as well as Pierre, Pietro, Pedro and other national variations.

Peter was a fisherman of Galilee, who denied knowing Christ three times during His trial, but later repented. Tradition tells us that he was crucified in A.D. 67, head down at his request because he said he was not worthy to suffer the same death as Jesus, and his tomb is under the high altar of St. Peter's in Rome. Many words and expressions derive from Peter's name: Eric Partridge alone devotes a page or so to them in his *A Dictionary of Slang*. The patron saint of fishermen and many other occupations connected with the sea gives us the standard English *peterman* for a fisherman and *peter boat* for a fishing boat with stem and stern alike. *Stormy petrels* also bear Peter's name, because the birds seem to be patting the waves with one foot and then the other in stormy weather, as though they were walking on the water. Actually they are flying close to the waves in search of surface-swimming food like small shrimp, but the birds reminded sailors of St. Peter walking upon the Lake of Gennersareth to join Jesus (*Matthew* 14:29). They were thus named *peterels*, a diminutive of the English Peter, in honor of the apostle and this came to be *petrel* in time. All petrels are regarded as the protectors of sailors and the harbingers of approaching storms. It is considered bad luck to kill one, for the birds were long thought to be the souls of drowned men; whenever one died, sailors believed a crew member would soon die to take its place. How *petrels* got the nickname *Mother Carey's chickens* is a mystery because no real Mother Carey has ever been found. But many etymologists uphold Ebenezer Brewer's theory that the words are a corruption of the Latin *Mater Cara* (Dear Mother), another name for the Virgin Mary. However, in the absence of evidence, Ernest Weekley's conclusion in *The Romance of Words* still seems best: "Mother Carey's chicken, probably a nautical corrpution of some old Spanish or Italian name; but, in spite of ingenious guesses, this lady's geneology remains as obscure as that of Davy Jones or the Jolly Roger."

Pharos, Inchcape Rock, Eddystone

Pharos has become a synonym for "lighthouse," but was originally one of the Seven Wonders of the World, a lighthouse built by Ptolomy II on the island of Pharos off Alexandria, Egypt, that was two hundred to six hundred feet high and could be seen forty-two miles away.

The *Inchcape Rock* was a dangerous rocky reef off Arbroath in the North Sea that had a bell on it to warn mariners of its dangers. A sea pirate named Ralph the Rover stole the bell and on his way home several weeks later was wrecked on the same rock.

The first *Eddystone* lighthouse, a wooden polygon one hundred feet high on a stone base, was built by engineer Henry Winstanley. Winstanley died in the structure when it was washed away in a 1703 storm.

Pieces of Eight, Doubloons, Cobs

Famous as pirate booty, *pieces of eight* were Spanish silver coins worth about a dollar, though they were frequently cut into bits to make smaller coins. Other famous Spanish coins were *half doubloons, quarter doubloons (pistols), one-eighth doubloons*, and *cobs*, silver coins of various worth irregularly cut from a silver bar, heated and stamped with the royal arms.

Pike

The *pike*, which takes its name from its *pike* or pointed head, is depicted in many religious paintings because of an old German tradition about the fish. After Christ's crucifixion all fishes but the pike were supposed to have dived under the water in terror. Out of curiosity the pike lifted its head from the water and observed the whole scene. Thus parts of the crucifixion are said to be recognizable on a pike's head, especially the cross, three nails and a sword.

Pinnace

Generally made of pine in days past, this little, light, usually two-masted sailing vessel takes its name from the Latin *pinus*, "pine tree."

Pipe Down

Pipe down was originally a nautical term referring to the dismissal command given a ship's crew to go belowdecks after a task was completed or a formation had ended. The command was transmitted by the bos'n's pipe or whistle on which the bos'n could sound notes representing many orders. Long a part of sea slang, *pipe down* came in the late nineteenth century to mean "shut up," because it got much quieter on deck when the crew obeyed the order to go below and because the phrase *pipe down* itself suggested someone piping down or making less noise.

Pirates and Privateers

Pirates, who take their name from the Latin *pirata*, meaning to attack, are sea raiders who operate without any authorization except that of their own greed and need. *Privateers*, however, who have been known since the thirteenth century, operate with the consent of a government, usually their own. *Privateers* were *privately* owned vessels that in England were licensed under Letter of Marque and Reprisal to capture enemy ships in time of war. A captain who had such authorization would not be charged with piracy. On the other hand, Sir Francis Drake, among the greatest of pirates, was not strictly a privateer, having preyed on Spanish ships before there was a declaration of war. Yet Queen Elizabeth I overlooked his crimes because part of his profits enriched her coffers. (See also *Buccaneer.*)

Pirogue

The Caribs called their dugout canoes *piraguas*, a word that French explorers changed slightly to *piroque* in the seventeenth century and passed on to the English, who called it *pirogue*.

Plimsoll Mark

"Coffin ships" sailors called the overloaded, undermanned, unseaworthy vessels that greedy owners sent to sea before Samuel Plimsoll, "the Sailors' Friend," appeared on the scene. Merchants generally profited handsomely even if such ships went down, for they were invariably overinsured, and the only ones who stood to lose were the hapless crews aboard them. That is, until Samuel Plimsoll (1824–1898), a brewery manager turned London coal dealer, made the British seaman's cause his own.

Shortly after being elected to Parliament from Derby in 1868, Plimsoll tried to pass a bill to improve the coffin-ship situation. His failure to do so prompted him to write a book, *Our Seamen*, which he published four years later. *Our Seamen* was largely a collection of dramatic stories about the hard lot of British sailors that its crusading author had obtained secondhand while haunting the waterfront to educate himself in maritime affairs. Though he was sued for libel by certain shipowners and forced to apologize in Parliament for revealing privileged information, Plimsoll's book accomplished its purpose. Its condemnation of shipowners and underwriters incensed the British people and enlisted their support. A royal commission was appointed in Parliament to investigate the murderous maritime situation and a reform bill was introduced. However, when Benjamin Disraeli announced in 1875 that the bill would be dropped, Plimsoll rose to his feet, shook his fist in the speaker's face and shouted that his fellow House members were villains. Again he was forced to apologize, yet due almost solely to his efforts reform was in the air. The following year saw passage of the Merchant Shipping Act, which provided for strict inspection of all vessels; this was followed by a number of similar maritime acts, one of which bore Plimsoll's name.

The *Plimsoll mark* or *line*, adopted in 1876, was named in honor of the reformer's suggestion that every vessel have a load line, a mark that indicates the limit to which a ship may be loaded. Located amidships on both sides of the ship, it is a circle with a horizontal line drawn through it showing the water level at maximum permitted loading. This innovation reformed shipping all over the globe, making Plimsoll's name world famous, although today American merchant ships use what are known as A.B.S. marks (American Bureau of Shipping): four lines amidships that show maximum loading conditions in freshwater and salt water during summer and winter. As for the Sailor's Friend, Plimsoll was reelected to Parliament in 1880, but resigned to become president of the Sailor's and Fireman's Union. He continued to agitate for further maritime reform and later visited America in an effort to change the bitter tone of American history books toward England. His mission was successful in many respects. His name is also remembered by *plimsolls*, rubber-soled shoes made of cloth with the rubber extending about halfway up the shoe, the line between cloth and rubber somewhat resembling a *Plimsoll mark*.

Plural Names for Marine Animals

Following are the proper plurals or collective names for a number of marine animals, enough at least to form the basis for a complete collection of your own.

A *bale* of turtles
A *bed* of clams or oysters
A *bevy* or *wedge* (flying) of swans
A *gam, school* or *pod* of whales
A *gaggle* of geese (on the ground)
A *herd* or *pod* of seals
A *hover* of trout
A *knot* of toads

A *paddling* of ducks (in the water)
A *school* of porpoises (or fish in general)
A *seige* of herring
A *shoal* of bass (or most fish species)
A *skein* of geese (in flight)
A *smack* of jellyfish
A *team* of ducks (in flight)

Pongo

In medieval legend the *pongo* was "a cross between a tiger and a sea-shark." It was a huge monster that devastated Sicily before it was slain by the three sons of St. George. The once common word is not found in most dictionaries, today, but for centuries it was applied not only to the terrible sea monster but also to a gorilla, of all things, probably because by some strange coincidence *pongo* is the name in a Bantu dialect for a large ape.

Pontoon

Pontus, the Greek god of the sea, gives his name to the *pontoon bridge*, a floating structure, as well as to the *pontoons* on seaplanes. The *pontoon hull* is a flat-bottomed hull with a squared-off bow; and the *pontoon lifeboat* is a lifeboat dependant for buoyancy on a watertight double bottom.

Port

About three centuries ago *port* began to replace *larboard* as the word for the left-hand side of a ship, probably because *larboard* was too easily confused in speech with *starboard*, the right-hand side. The word *port* here probably derives from port, a harbor. In the days when the steering gear was on the starboard (that is, steer-board) side, a vessel almost always had to tie up at the dock with her left side toward the port.

Portholes

All windows on a ship are called *portholes*, even though half of them are on the starboard side. This is because in early times the only windows on, a ship were the *port holes* for guns. When windows were later added for the comfort of sailors sleeping below, they too were called portholes.

Portuguese Man-of-war

Physalia pelagica was derisively named the *Portuguese man-of-war* by the English in the eighteenth century, when the once powerful Portuguese Navy had gone into a state of decline. The designation is a strange one, for small as it is, the *Portuguese man-of-war* can be deadly. Actually not an individual animal but a colony of highly specialized polyps, it has tentacles up to fifty feet long which discharge a toxic substance that has painfully stung, paralyzed and even killed swimmers coming into contact with them. With its red saillike crest it does resemble a little ship, but either afloat or beached it should be more an object inspiring respect than ridicule.

Posh

A favorite story about *posh* says that it is an acronym for *p*ort outward, *s*tarboard *h*ome. British civil servants traveling to India on the Peninsular and Oriental Steam Navigation Company line supposedly liked to have their accommodations on the port side of the ship leaving home and on the starboard side coming back as these locations were shady and away from the weather. According to the tale, such first-class or *posh* staterooms became a synonym for anything elegant or sophisticated, but, unfortunately, the famous P&O line has no record of such an expression ever being used. This doesn't prove that the ingenious story isn't true, but the term is just as likely a contraction of "polished" or "polish." *Posh* is first recorded in 1897 as meaning "a dandy" and so may also be a corruption of the slang term *pot* ("big"), a person of importance. A corruption of the Scottish *tosh*, "neat and trim," isn't out of the question, either.

To Pour Oil on Troubled Waters

Pour oil on any waters today and you'll stir up a storm among ecologists rather than soothe or calm a situation by tact and diplomacy, which is the figurative meaning of the above phrase. The ancients, Pliny and Plutarch among them, believed that oil poured on stormy waters reduced the waves to a calm and allowed a vessel to ride through a storm. The Venerable Bede says in his *Historia Ecclesiastica Gentis Anglorum* (731) that Bishop Aidan, an Irish monk, gave a priest, who was to deliver King Oswy's bride to him, holy oil to pour on the sea if the waves became threatening; his miraculous oil would stop the wind from blowing. A storm did blow up and the priest saved the ship and the future queen by following this advice. Later, Benjamin Franklin mentioned the practice of pouring oil on troubled waters in a letter and it is said that the captains of American whaling vessels sometimes ordered oil poured on stormy' waters. Oil spills today, however, trouble the waters, polluting them and killing wildlife. In fact, men have even suffocated in oil slicks, as did the crew of the sinking tanker *Usworth* in 1934.

Proctophilus winchilli

It is said that while they were fishing in the Gulf of Lower California, Nobel Prize winner John Steinbeck and his friend Doc Ricketts noticed a little fish that lived in the cloaca of the sea cucumber and that kept darting in and out of the creature's anus. They named the hitherto unrecorded fish *Proctophilus winchilli*, after Walter Winchell. It is probably the only fish named after a gossip columnist— and probably one too many as far as Winchell was concerned.

PT Boat

Prohibition rather than war prompted the invention of *PT boats*, which were originally used by rum runners because the little boats could outspeed the Coast Guard cutters of the day. Their inventor submitted their design to the Navy during World War II and they were introduced as *Patrol Torpedo* boats, although their size and annoyance to the enemy caused them to be dubbed "mosquito" boats as well. John F. Kennedy's *PT-109* was cut in half by a Japanese destroyer in the Pacific and Kennedy heroically saved several of his crew members.

Q-boats

British *Q-boats*—warships disguised as merchant ships—destroyed many a German U-boat during World War II. "Panic parties," men who abandoned ship when fired upon, were launched by these decoys, tempting the U-boats to come closer so that concealed guns manned by hidden crews could blast them out of the water. Their name, deriving from an abbreviation of the Latin *quaere*, "inquire" (as the U-boats did), *Q-boats* were also called *hush-hush* ships and *mystery ships*. So odd were they in construction that they were often nicknamed H.M.S. *Outrageous, Spurious, Unspeakable, Obnoxious*, et cetera.

Quadrant

Associated primarily with navigation at sea and astronomy since its development centuries ago, the *quadrant* is an instrument properly having the form of a graduated quarter circle that is used for making angular measurements, especially for taking altitudes in navigation. It takes its name from the Latin *quadrant*, "fourth part" or quarter.

Quaker Guns

The dummy guns on ships have long been called *Quaker guns* in allusion to the Quakers' opposition to war and killing. As far back as 1830, an American naval officer wrote: "Our six iron six-pounders and six *quakers* [wooden guns], were, like millenial lion and lamb, lying down together in the hold."

Quarantine

In naval terms a *quarantine* is a secluded berth in a port where a ship infected with a contagious disease is kept for a certain length of time. Ships have been quarantined in the United States for every disease from measles to the dread bubonic plague. *Quarantine* itself ultimately derives from the Italian *quarantina*, "forty," in reference

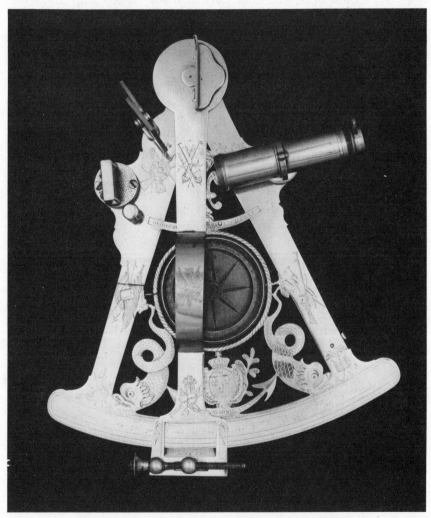

A brass Hadley quadrant, finely engraved for presentation to Louis XVI in 1786

PEABODY MUSEUM OF SALEM

to the forty days that travelers from other countries were isolated during the Middle Ages if they had come from a plague-stricken country.

Quarterdeck
A vessel's *quarterdeck* is that part of a full-rigged ship abaft the mainmast on the spar deck. Today the quarterdeck is usually the part of the main deck adjacent to the starboard gangway where distinguished visitors are received on any ship.

The Queen
"The Queen, God bless her!," frequently abbreviated to *the Queen*, is the Loyal Toast to Her Majesty's health often made in British naval wardrooms. It is customarily drunk while seated because King William IV, "The Sailor King," is said to have hit his head on a wardroom beam while rising to make the toast.

Quoddy Boat
These double-ended keelboats with a gaff mainsail and sometimes a jib set on a detachable bowsprit were long used for lobstering and fishing along the Maine coast. They take their name from the Passama*quoddy* Bay between New Brunswick, Canada, and Maine, where they first were used.

R *Months*

Many people still believe that oysters are safe to eat only during months containing an *R*. So common is this canard that it has been commemorated in the poem "The Man Who Dared" by Stoddard King: "Let's sing a song of glory to Themistocles O'Shea,/Who ate a dozen oysters on the second day of May." The U.S. Bureau of Commerical Fisheries has been trying to dispel this old wive's tale for years, but the rumor persistently finds its way into print, in one guise or another, and the real reason for its long life is never given.

Many of the origins of the hoary story have been lost in time. It is first mentioned in literature in William Butler's *Dyet's Dry Dinner* (1599) where Butler wrote: "It is unreasonable and unwholesome in all months that have an R in their name to eat an oyster." The *R* myth does derive partly from those days when poor refrigeration resulted in spoilage during "those melancholy hot months that are spelled without an *R*," as another writer put it. But more important is the fact that the flat European oyster (*Ostrea edulis*), only one of the more than one hundred oyster species, is definitely *not* desirable as human food during the non-*R* months. *Ostrea edulis* is unique in that its young are retained by the mothers until tiny shells are developed; the presence of these gritty shells while it's spawning make the European oyster undesirable in the summer. Such is not the case with American oysters (*Crassostrea virginica*, Atlantic coast, and *Ostrea lurida*, Pacific coast), which do not incubate their young but disperse them in the water where they are fertilized outside the organism. American oysters can be eaten safely at any time of the year. Although no mollusk is at its best during the torrid summer months, this is no reason for oyster markets to practically shut down from May to September. In point of fact, American oysters reach the peak of perfection in May and June, months without an *R* in them, when they are fatter and taste better because they are beginning to store glycogen in preparation for summer spawning. During summer and early autumn, oyster flavor declines. Due to the expenditure of the glycogen, the meat becomes skimpier and the nectar watery. Ironically, the traditional oyster harvesttime is still in the fall because the demand is seasonal and the prices highest at this time.

Red Herring

Strong-smelling red herring—herring that have been cured and become red in color—were used by escaping criminals in the seventeenth century. These hunted men would drag a red herring across a trail to make bloodhounds lose the human scent they had been following. This practice inspired the popular expression *to drag a red herring across the trail* and the more recent shortened term *red herring,* which means evading an issue by dragging in something irrelevant to the matter.

The Red Sea

The Red Sea was so named by the Romans (*Mare rubrum*), but they took the designation from an old Semitic name whose meaning is not certain, so no one knows the real reason why the sea is called red.

Regatta

There is no complicated derivation behind the word *regatta.* A *regatta* was first, back in the seventeenth century, a race between gondolas on the Grand Canal in Venice. This Venetian dialect word translates as "a strife or contention or struggling for mastery." The first English *regatta,* or yacht race, was held on the River Thames on June 23, 1775. So popular did *regattas* become in the nineteenth century that the word *regatting* became as common as *hunting* or *fishing.*

Remora

Roman sailors believed that the little shark *remora* (*Remora remora*) fastened itself to their sailing vessels and slowed them down, delaying them, so they named the fish *remora,* or "delayer." In nature the remora attaches itself to the undersides of sharks, whales, swordfish and even tuna by means of its highly efficient suction disk, which is actually a greatly modified first and spiny dorsal fin. Not only does it hitch a free ride, but it also eats pieces of food dropped by the host fish. The remora does do some good, however, by acting as a cleaner fish and removing parasites from its host's hide.

Requiem Shark

Tiger sharks and other tropical sharks of the family Carcharhinidae are often called *requiem sharks*, their name coming from the French word *requin* for shark. In 1887 the pseudonymous sailor Sinbad ex-

The regatta was a popular nineteenth-century sport
LIBRARY OF CONGRESS

163

plained the derivation of the French word in a book he wrote about sharks:

> The French name for shark is *requin*. This word is probably derived from the Latin *requiem*, and signifies that if a man fall into the sea among sharks, his comrades may repeat for him the usual prayers for the dead. It is seldom, if ever, that a man who is so luckless as to fall amongst sharks appears again; a shriek is heard, a moving mass is seen under the surface and a fin above it; the next wave that breaks against the shipside is crimsoned, and the horror-stricken seamen know that their messmate has gone to that place from which no traveler returns.

To Rile

To rile, deriving from the Old French *roiller*, "to roll or flow" (like a stream), was originally an English dialect word common in Norfolk that meant to muddy the water by stirring it up. This process disturbed the water and suggested *rile's* modern meaning of to annoy or make angry.

Round Robin

Mutineers aboard ships often resorted to the *round robin* so that no leader could be singled out if they failed. The *round robin* was originally a petition, its signatures arranged in a circular form to disguise the order of signing. Most probably it takes its name from the *ruban rond*, "round ribbon," in seventeenth-century France, where government officials devised a method of signing their petitions of grievances on ribbons that were attached to the documents in a circular form. In that way no signer could be accused of signing the document first and having his head chopped off for instigating trouble. *Ruban rond* later became *round robin* in English and the custom continued in the British Navy, where petitions of grievances were signed as if the signatures were spokes of a wheel radiating from its hub. Today a *round robbin* usually means a sports tournament where all of the contestants play each other at least once and losing a match doesn't result in immediate elimination.

Rudderless; Who Won't Be Ruled by the Rudder Must Be Ruled by the Rock

Rudderless, in reference to the absence of a ship's rudder, since the early nineteenth century has figuratively meant "without guidance or control." The nautical saying *Who won't be ruled by the rudder must be ruled by the rock* isn't found in the *Oxford English Dictionary, Bartlett's Familiar Quotations* or any other major collection of quotations. Dating back at least a century, it means "those who won't listen to reason must bear the consequences, like a ship that runs upon a rock if it will not answer the helm."

Rummage Sale

The French word *arrimage*, related to our word "arrange," meant "loading a cargo ship" as early as the fourteenth century. Sometimes cargo from the *arrimage* was damaged during the voyage and warehouses held special sales of these damaged items, sales that were at first called *arrimage* sales and then *rummage* sales. *Rummage* thus came to mean any damaged goods and finally any goods low in quality, including the used clothing and other items sold at charity rummage sales.

Run the Gauntlet

Originally the *gauntlet* in this expression was spelled *gantlope*. It derives from the Swedish word *gattloppe*, from *gat*, "a narrow path," and *loppe*, "run" (akin to our *lope, elope* and *gallop*), which literally meant "a running of the narrow path." *Gatloppe* was the name of a punishment that originated in the Swedish Army. A soldier found guilty of a serious offense was forced to strip naked and run between two rows of his comrades, each of whom struck him with a whip, switch or even sword as he ran. The length of the rows depended on the severity of his offense and were shorter, of course, aboard ship.

The English observed the use of this punishment by the Germans during the Thirty Years War (1618–1648) and saw American Indians inflict a similar punishment on captives with war clubs. They called the torture, which often resulted in maiming, *running the gantlope* at first, nasalizing the Swedish word *gatloppe*, but later further corrupted the key word in the phrase to *gauntlet*, probably because of

165

its resemblance to the English *gauntlet* for glove. Today the expression means to encounter trouble on all sides, to be severely attacked or criticized. The confusion between this *gauntlet* and the *gauntlet* that is a glove has led some writers to spell the punishment *gantlet.* In any case, both words are still pronounced the same.

To Sail Under False Colors

Pretending to be something you aren't, to be a hypocrite. We all know the origins of this one from movie swashbucklers, where the pirate ship at the moment of attack lowers its friendly or neutral flag and hoists the deadly skull and crossbones. The unwritten law of the sea, of course, required that all ships display their true flags or colors so that they could be recognized as friend or foe, but the Jolly Roger was by its nature exempt.

St. Elmo's Fire

"Look aloft!" cried Starbuck. "The corpusants! the corpusants!"

All the yard-arms were tipped with a pallid fire; and touched at each tri-pointed lightning-rod-end with three tapering white flames, each of the three tall masts was silently burning in that sulphurous air, like three gigantic wax tapers before an altar."

Melville's description of corposants in *Moby-Dick* reveals the superstitious awe with which mariners regarded these luminous discharges of electricity that extend into the atmosphere from projecting objects. Corposants, the word deriving from the Portuguese *corpo santo*, "holy body," are better known nautically as *St. Elmo's fire*, and were believed by sailors to be a portent of bad weather. St. Erasmus, the patron saint of Neapolitan sailors, was a fourth-century Italian bishop whose name became corrupted to St. Elmo. An Italian legend tells us that he was rescued from drowning by a sailor and as a reward promised to ever after display a warning light for mariners whenever a storm was approaching. *St. Elmo's fire* does not involve enough discharge of electricity to be considered dangerous. The jets of fire are also seen on the wings of aircraft, mountain tops, church steeples, on the horns of cattle, and blades of grass, and even around the heads of people, where it is said that they merely cause a tingling sensation. In ancient times *St. Elmo's fire* was called *Castor and Pollux*, for the twin sons of Zeus and Leda in Roman mythology, and a single burst of fire was called a *Helen*, for the twins' sister. A Helen was said to be a warning that the worst of a storm was yet to come, while two lights, *Castor and Pollux*, supposedly meant that the worst had passed. This has given rise to the theory that *St. Elmo* may be a corruption of *Helen* instead of *St. Erasmus.* Still another suggestion is that *St. Elmo* is a corruption of *St. Anselm* of Lucca.

To Sally a Ship

To *sally* a ship is to roll her by assembling the crew all on one side, then signaling them to rush together to the other side. By repeating the signal at certain intervals, the ship can be made to roll. During the age of sail, *sally* was also a common expression for the continuous rising and falling or the swinging or bounding motion of a ship at sea. The word derives from the Middle French *saillir*, "to rush forward," which comes from the Latin *salire*, "to leap."

"Save a Sailor!"

An old naval superstition has it that when a glass "rings" in a bar or at a table, a sailor will be drowned—unless a finger is placed on the glass to stop the ringing and someone cries out, *"Save a sailor!"*

Schillerlocken

A German fish dish named after the hair of a poet, *Schillerlocken* is curled chips of smoked fish commemorating the curly locks of the poet Johann Christoph Friedrich von Schiller. Schiller (1759–1805) was one of the founders of modern German literature; only Johann von Goethe overshadowed him in his time. Forced to become a doctor while serving in military school against his wishes, Schiller finally rebelled and lived as a fugitive for a time. He was a poet, dramatist, historian and philosopher and many of his ballads became German classics as well. Schiller was a great favorite of the

*Cruises along the Maine coast are available aboard the
schooner* Stephen Taber, *1871, the oldest documented
sailing vessel in continuous service in the United States*

German people, and the wide popularity of his works led to the affectionate word made from his surname and *Locken* ("curl").

Schooner

"Oh, how she *scoons*!" an onlooker is supposed to have exclaimed
when Captain Andrew Robinson of Gloucester, Massachusetts,
launched the first vessel of this kind back in 1713 and she glided
gracefully over the water. Captain Robinson, overhearing the remark, called his ship a *scooner,* which came to be mispelled

schooner over the years. The word *scoon* itself probably derives from the Scottish *scon*, to skip a flat stone over the water, as in the game *ducks and drakes*.

Scow

Scow is another nautical word born in America; its parents were the Dutch *schouw*, a large flat-bottomed pole boat or river boat, and a mispronunciation, which turned *schouw* into *scow*. Usually serving as a ferryboat or lighter in the beginning, the scow first entered the language in the mid-seventeenth century and is first recorded in 1669: "The Governor hath given me Orders . . . to provyde a scow to help ye souldiers in their provision of fire wood." *To scow* meant to cross a river by scow and America has since known *cattle, dumping, ferry, mud, oyster, snag, sand, steam, stone-trading* and *garbage scows*.

Scrimshaw

Sailors on long voyages in whaling days would often spend their spare time carefully carving whalebone, shells or ivory into decorative and useful objects, ranging from clothespins to elaborate canes and jewelry boxes. This intricate work was called *scrimshaw*, a word whose origins are rather vague. *Webster*'s traces *scrimshaw* to the French *escrimer*, to fight with a sword, in the sense "to make flourishes," while other dictionaries suggest *scrimshank*, English military slang for "to evade duty, be a shirker." Just as many authorities believe the word comes from the proper name Scrimshaw, referring to some once illustrious sailor-carver noted for his craftsmanship. But our Scrimshaw, if he did exist, hasn't been identified. *Scrimshaw* work was also called *skrimshander* and today it can mean any good piece of mechanical work.

Scrod

Scrod derives from the Middle Dutch *schrode*, meaning a strip or shred. In New England, scrod may be immature cod or haddock weighing one and a half to two and a half pounds. Sometimes the term is applied to cusk of about the same weight, or to pollack weighing one and a half to four pounds. When fishermen use the word, they are usually referring to gutted small haddock.

Scuba

All fanciful stories about the word to the contrary, *scuba* is simply an acronym standing for "*s*elf-*c*ontained *u*nderwater *b*reathing *a*pparatus." Popular since World War II, *scuba diving* has enabled millions to see underwater sights previously the province of a few thousand professional divers.

Sailors often made elaborate scrimshaw like these to while away their spare time

171

Scuttlebutt

The Old French word *escoutilles*, corrupted to *scuttle* in English, first meant a hatch on a ship, then meant the hole or hatchway in the hatch, and finally was used as a verb meaning to open a hole in a ship in order to sink or *scuttle* her. The cask or butt of drinking water on ships was called a *scuttlebutt* because it was a *butt* with a square hole cut in it, and since sailors exchanged gossip when they gathered at the *scuttlebutt* for a drink of water, *scuttlebutt* became U.S. Navy slang for gossip or rumors, in about 1935.

Seabees

Special Navy construction battalions of World War II built airstrips or runways on many Pacific islands, among other duties. Their name, *Seabees*, is a phonetic acronym from the initials CB, Construction Battalion. The *C* was spelled "sea" because they were Navy men.

Seagoing Bellhops

A contemptuous name given to marines by sailors, in reference to their colorful uniforms, *seagoing bellhops* is an expression still heard occasionally among Navy men. It probably originated in England during the late nineteenth century.

Sea Horse

Among the most unfishlike of fish, the little sea horse, or *Hippocampus*, as he is known scientifically, has a head and arched neck very horselike in outline and swims upright. Sea horses are also unusual in their breeding habits. During mating, the female's eggs are fertilized by the male as they are shed, but the female deposits them in the male's abdomen. The male's pelvic fins are converted into a large incubating pouch that holds the eggs and he carries them about until they are ready to hatch, appearing as if *he* were pregnant. Twenty-five days or so later, the world's only "pregnant father" bends over as if he has a bellyache and, one by one, hundreds of baby sea horses begin popping out of his pouch.

Sea Lawyer

An old nautical dictionary (1867) defines a *sea lawyer* as "an idle litigious long-shorer, more given to questioning orders than to obeying them. One of the pests of the navy as well as the mercantile marine." This term for an argumentative seaman or nautical nuisance given to questioning naval laws, rules and regulations is still used and the type is still with us for better or worse. A good example is the officer responsible for the mutiny against Captain Queeg in Herman Wouk's *The Caine Mutiny*.

Because it is so clever and cunning, the tiger shark is also called the *sea lawyer*, as is the gray, or mangrove, snapper.

Sea Urchin

The English, who have often been poor at spelling French words, stumbled badly over the synonym for "hedgehog" that the Normans brought to England, spelling *hurcheon* a number of ways before finally settling on *urchin*. They called the hedgehog an *urchin* for a time and also applied the name *urchin* to a mischievous child, because the urchin or hedgehog was popularly believed to be a mischievous elf in disguise. People eventually stopped using *urchin* as a synonym for "hedgehog," but not for an impish child. Neither was the name *sea urchin* abandoned. This spiny creature was originally

The male sea horse, which incubates the female's eggs
in its pouch, finally expels the youngster out into the sea
SMITHSONIAN INSTITUTION

173

named for its resemblance to the urchin or hedgehog and once was called the *sea hedgehog.*

Seiche

This is a long wave that rhythmically sloshes back and forth as if in a bathtub as it reflects off opposite ends of an enclosed body of water (usually a bay) when it is disturbed by storms, winds or tsunami. In Los Angeles Harbor, one of the few major harbors that have seiching or surging problems, seiches cause big ships to move as much as ten feet, to strain at or snap their mooring lines, and cause damage to piles and to the ships themselves. *Seiche*, a French word, is generally pronounced *saysh*, though people in some regions pronounce it to rhyme with "beach."

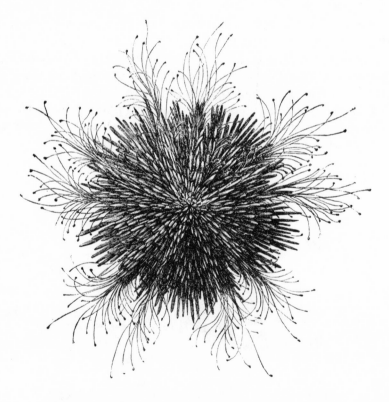

A New England sea urchin
MEYER'S ANIMAL LEXICON, *1895*

To Set One's Cap At

A rather unlikely theory traces this expression to a French saying meaning to set the head (or cap) of a ship at a particular point and sail straight for it. The phrase more likely goes back to the eighteenth century, a time when ladies wore light muslin caps indoors as well as out. When a suitor came to call, a young woman would naturally put on her best cap and wear it at the most fetching angle in order to impress her man and win a husband. This was called *setting one's cap at* or *for* a man, an expression still occasionally heard in a time when better heating has made such headgear obsolete.

The Seven Seas

Nine out of ten people will tell you that there are seven seas on earth and many may even name the North and South Atlantic, North and South Pacific, the Arctic and Antarctica, and the Indian Ocean as these seven. But in truth, counting the oceans alone, there are more like seventy-five seas than seven around the world. Not including great salt lakes such as the Dead Sea and the Coral Sea, which aren't technically parts of oceans, these would include: the Adriatic; Aegean; Alborán; Amundsen; Andaman; Arabian; Arafura; Azov; Balearic; Bali; Baltic; Banda; Barents; Bellingshausen; Bering; Bismarck; Black; Caribbean; Caspian; Celebes; Ceram; Chukchi; Crete; East China; East Siberian; Euboean; Flores; Greenland; Halmahera; Hebrides; Inland; Ionian; Irish; Japan; Java; Kara; Labrador; Laccadive; Laptev; Lincohn; Mediterranean; Mindanao; Molucca; North; Norwegian; Okhotsk; Philippine; Red; Ross; Sargasso; Savu; Scotia; Scottish; Sibuyan; Solomon; South China; Sulu; Suō; Tasman; Timor; Tyrrhenian; Vermilion; Visayan; Wadden; Wandels; Weddell; White and Yellow seas. Know any others that qualify?

Shaddock, Grapefruit, Pomelo

The *shaddock*, or *pomelo*, is the ancestor of the grapefruit and reached Europe in about the middle of the twelfth century from the Malay Archipelago. It was called the Adam's apple at first and didn't receive its common name until a Captain Shaddock, a seventeenth-century English voyager, brought its seed from the East Indies to Barbados, where it was grown extensively. The grapefruit (*Citrus paradisi*) is either a mutation of the thicker-skinned shaddock (*C.*

grandis), or a cross between the *shaddock* and sweet orange. It was developed in the West Indies and was given its name because it often grows in clusters like grapes. To further complicate matters, the *shaddock* is sometimes called the *forbidden fruit* and the grapefruit the *pomelo* in different parts of the world. The pink grapefruit was developed in Florida, as was the seedless variety.

To Shanghai

Shanghai here is a shortening of the expression *to ship a man to Shanghai*. American sailors first used the words to describe how press gangs got them drunk, drugged them, or blackjacked them and forced them in service aboard a ship in need of a crew. At the time Shanghai, a long way from home, was a leading Chinese shipping port, and many a *shanghaied* sailor did wind up there. The term became so common in the nineteenth century that it was applied to anyone seized or forced to work unwillingly.

Shark

Ironically enough, sea *sharks* take their name from land sharks, rather than the other way around. The German *Schurke*, "a greedy parasite," gives us the word *shark* and German sailors applied this term to the sea creature, no doubt having the greedy land shark in mind when they did so. British sailors brought the word home in about 1569, the same year that English mariner John Hawkins exhibited a huge shark in London. *Shark* was quickly adopted to describe both the killer fish and his human counterpart. (See Shrimp, page 180.)

She *for a Ship*

Even a *man*-of-war is called *she* in naval parlance. In all Romance languages the word for *ship* is in the feminine gender. Ships were therefore called *she* by sailors when their proper names weren't used. Though English nouns do not have gender, this habit of seafaring men from other countries was probably emulated by Englishmen.

Shark fishing in the early nineteenth century
LOUIS FIGUER, THE OCEAN WORLD, 1896

Sheet Anchor

This name for an emergency anchor has confused etymologists for many years. The best bet is that the word *sheet* here derives from *shoot.* According to this theory, the device was first called a *shoot anchor* because when an emergency came, it had to be "shot" out, that is, dropped quickly. In any event, no sheets or sails were involved.

Ship

The etymology of ship can be traced back to the Old English *scip* or "shape," evidence that the word *ship* arose when a ship was "no more than a trunk of a tree scooped out and *shaped* to enable it to glide safely and smoothly through the water," according to one nautical authority.

Ship Names

There has never been any universal system for naming ships. While the British preferred frightening names like *Invincible, Devastation, Shark* and *Hyena* for their warships, the Japanese have always liked romantic names such as *Siranui* (Phosphorescent Foam) and *Kasumi* (Mist of Flowers). No rigid logic seems ever to have been at work here, although the U.S. Navy did institute a comprehensive system during World War II, prescribing that the classes of ships be named in a certain manner (battleships after states, cruisers after cities, et cetera). Many ship names have been used scores of times. The revolutionary British *Dreadnought* of 1906, for example, was the eighth ship in English naval history to bear that name, and others have used it since. And don't forget that sailors on the most strictly disciplined ships often called them by entirely different names: The *Missouri*, for example, was sometimes called the *Misery*; the *Brooklyn* was called the *Teakettle*; while the *Salt Lake City* was often called the *Swayback Marie*! In 1982 the U.S. Navy broke an old tradition by naming a ship after a living person, Admiral Hyman G. Rickover, who pioneered the nuclear submarine fleet.

Ship of Fools

Written long before Katherine Anne Porter's *Ship of Fools*, Sebastian Brandt's famous *Narrenschiff*, or *Ship of Fools*, published in 1494, had as its theme the shipping of fools of all kinds from their native land of Swabia to the fictional land of Fools. The various fools were introduced in the book by classes and reproved for their folly. In fifteenth-century Germany, there were real *Narrenschiffs*. These most unusual ships were riverboats used to imprison the insane and thus clear city streets of them. Real ships of fools plied up and down the Rhine carrying their cargoes of madmen, who were thought to have lost their souls and were supposed to sail back and forth until they became sane again. However, most of them died aboard these hell ships, which had no destination but death.

Shipping Lanes

U.S. Navy Lieutenant Matthew Fontaine Maury recommended "lanes" or "strips" for ships traveling westbound in the Atlantic after the U.S. mail steamer *Arctic* collided with the French steamer *Vesta* in 1854. The recommended lanes were given in his book *Sailing Directions*, which was published the following year. These lanes became the building blocks for today's complex, internationally approved seasonal routes.

Shiver Me Timbers!

This phrase is, as one writer claims, a cricket expression "referring to the scattering of wickets, for which timber is a slang substitute." But it goes back much further. Originally *timbers!* was an eighteenth-century nautical slang exclamation with no real meaning to it: "My timbers! what lingo he'd coil and belay." Novelist Captain Frederick Marryat then embroidered the oath, making it *Shiver my timbers!* in *Jacob Faithful* (1834), an ejaculation you can be sure no sailor used before this.

The Shortest- and Longest-Named Bodies of Water

A river flowing into the Pacific Ocean from Devils Lake in Lincoln City, Oregon, is called the D, which is the shortest-named body of water anywhere. The longest named body of water is located near Webster, Massachusetts, and is called Lake Webster by almost everyone. However, its official, Indian-derived name is composed of forty letters and fourteen syllables, translating into English as, "You fish on your side; we fish on our side; nobody fish in the middle." Should anyone want to try pronouncing it, the lake is called: Chargogagogmanchaugagogchaubunagungamaug.

A Shotten Herring

Worthless or spiritless persons have been called *shotten herring* since Shakespeare's time because they resemble such fish. Shotten herring are herring that have "shot off" or ejected their spawn and are weak, tired and worthless.

Show a Leg; Shake a Leg

Nautical in origin and from the early nineteenth century, *show a leg* means to get up from bed, to hurry or be alert. One version of its birth says that when the bos'n's mate on sailing ships woke up the crew in the morning, he cried, "Show a leg, show a leg or a stocking!" At that time, according to the story, women were allowed to be on board ship, ostensibly as sailors' wives, and "a leg in a stocking put over the side of a hammock indicated that the occupant was a woman, who was allowed to remain until the men had cleared out." A more prosaic and reasonable account says the bos'n cried, "Come on, all you sleepers! Hey! Show a leg and put a stocking on it." *Shake a leg*, meaning "hurry," may derive from this earlier phrase, for both are nautical expressions and no better explanation has been given.

Shrimp

Contrary to popular belief, small people are not called shrimps because they resemble the shellfish in size. As with *sharks* (see page 176), it is the other way around. The common little European species *Crago vulgaris* was named shrimp from the Middle English word *shrimpe*, which meant a small, puny person.

Sirens

Often represented as birds with the heads of women in mythology, the Sirens were the three daughters of the Greek sea god Phorcu (Achelous). Perched on their pleasant island, they lured mariners to death, the sailors enchanted by Siren song and crashing their ships against the rocks. In rare instances they could be defeated, as when Orpheus, the legendary poet, outwitted the Sirens by playing his spellbinding lyre over the sound of their song.

Six of One and a Half Dozen of Another
This expression may have been invented by Captain Frederick Marryat in *The Pirates and the Three Cutters* (1836), or else it was naval slang that the author repeated. It apparently arose from no specific situation and means "nothing to choose between," "one and the same," simply because "six" and "a half dozen" are identical. *Arcades ambo*, a similar phrase, means two persons having the same tastes or habits in common. It comes from Vergil's seventh eclogue: "Ambo florentes aetabibus, Arcades ambo" ("Both in the flower of youth, Arcadians both").

To Skate on Thin Ice
The allusion is to skating over ice so thin that it won't bear the skater's weight if he slows down, a form of skating where safety is in speed, as Ralph Waldo Emerson said. The sport, common among youngsters wherever there are ponds, lakes, bays or rivers, was once called "tickledy-bendo" in New England—probably because you just "tickled" the ice, skated over it so lightly that you barely bent it. The metaphor *skating on thin ice* means that someone is taking chances, or is conducting himself in a manner verging on the questionable, dangerous or indelicate.

Skipper
Scip meant ship in Old English and *scipper* meant a ship's captain. By 1390 the English were pronouncing the latter word *skipper* and using it for the captain of a small merchant vessel. It now refers to the captain of any ship.

The Skipper Swallows the Anchor
Used especially on steamship liners, this nautical expression means that the captain or skipper of a ship has retired. *The skipper swal-*

lows the anchor dates back to about the late nineteenth century, and is sometimes used to indicate death has come as well.

Skyscraper
The name *skyscraper* was bestowed upon the first building to employ steel-skeleton construction, the Chicago office of the Home Insurance Company, built in 1883. But American journalists borrowed the word from the triangular sails that had long been used high on the masts of sailing vessels, sails that scraped against the sky. William Le Baron Jenney, the architect who built the Home Insurance Building, wasn't the first to use iron building frameworks, but his ten-story structure, the tallest of its day, was the first that used iron frameworks to support both the outside and inside walls.

Slush Fund
James Fenimore Cooper made mention of a *slush fund* in one of his sea novels back in 1842. The expression has its origins in the surplus fat or grease from fried salt pork, a staple food on nineteenth-century ships, which was usually sold in port after a voyage. The money raised from the *slush* was put into a general *fund* used to purchase little luxuries for the crew. These were the first *slush funds*, but by 1866 the term was being applied to a contingent fund set aside by Congress from an operating budget. In another decade or so, *slush fund* took on its present usual meaning of a secret fund used for bribes or other corrupt practices, such as buying votes.

Small Fry
Harriet Beecher Stowe introduced *small fry* ("smaller fry") to describe children in *Uncle Tom's Cabin*, but *fry* was used in this sense as early as 1697. Both expressions refer to the *fry*, or young, of salmon, herring and other fish. The word derives from the Norse *frae*, "seed," meaning the berry or seedlike masses of eggs these fish produce.

A Snail's Pace

A snail's pace has meant "exceedingly slow" since at least 1592, when the expression was collected in a book of English proverbs, but until recently no one knew just how exceedingly slow that was. Recent studies have shown that snails travel at about two feet an hour, or one mile every three months or so. The snail has a good excuse, though: the weight of his shell to his body corresponds to a 129-pound man carrying a shed of some 200 pounds!

Snorkel

Introduced during World War II, the *snorkel* was at first only a retractable tube that ventilated a sub cruising slightly below the surface. The snorkel took its name from the German *Schnorchel,* "air intake." After the war, *snorkel* became better known as a tube one breathes through while swimming facedown in the water or slightly below the surface.

Soldier's Breeze or Wind

> The wind was what is called at sea a 'soldier's wind,' that is, blowing so that the ships could lie either way, so as to run out or into the harbour.
> —CAPTAIN FREDERICK MARRAYAT, *Peter Simple*

A contemptuous regard for landlubbers is reflected in this nineteenth-century term for a wind that is equally forcible going or coming. In other words when the wind is about abeam going out and coming back, it takes little ability to sail—even a soldier could do it.

Son of a Gun

Though in recent times this has been a euphemism for the much stronger *son of a bitch,* or even a term of affectionate regard between friends ("You old son of a gun!"), the expression did not start out that way. It dates back to the early 1800s and was just a little less pejorative than *son of a bitch,* or *whore,* which came into the language at about the same time. In the early nineteenth century, *son of a gun* meant "a sailor's bastard," but it proceeded to become more innocuous with the passing of time. *The Sailor's Word-book* (1867), written by British Navy Admiral William Henry Smyth, attempts to explain the expression's origins, but bear in mind that the book was written a long time after the term was born: "An epithet conveying contempt in a slight degree, and originally applied to boys born afloat, when women were permitted to accompany their husbands to sea; one admiral declared he literally was thus cradled, under the breast of a gun-carriage."

Son of a Sea Cook

It should be explained that *son of a sea cook*, which can mean either a "good guy" or a "mean SOB," depending on the context, really has little to do with the sea. At least no sea cook had any hand in it. It seems that the earliest American settlers appropriated the word *s'quenk*, for "skunk," from the Indians around the Massachusetts Bay Colony, pronouncing it *sea-konk*. Thus, a *son of a see-konk* was first a stinking son of a skunk. Because *see-konk* sounded something like "sea cook" it came to be pronounced "sea cook" long after the Indian word was forgotten. The fact that sea cooks were often can-

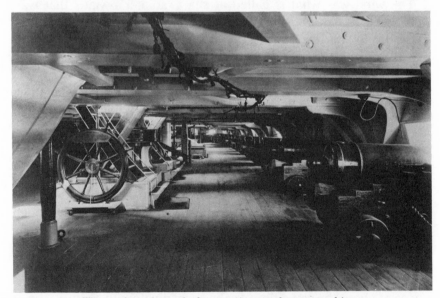

The starboard gun deck on a nineteenth-century ship
THE COMPLETE ENCYCLOPEDIA OF ILLUSTRATION

tankerous old men (but did dispense the food) probably reinforced the term's present ambivalent meaning.

SOS, CQD, Mayday

The universal distress call *SOS* doesn't stand for "Save Our Ship," "Save Our Souls" or "Stop Other Signals." The letters, adopted in 1908 by international agreement, actually mean nothing at all and were only chosen because they are so simple for a wireless operator to remember and transmit in Morse Code—three dits (dashes), three dahs (dots) and three dits (... --- ...). Another telegraph symbol for requesting aid was *CQD* (*CQ*, the general call alerting other ships that a message follows, and the *D* standing for "danger"). But these letters, proposed after the *Titanic* sank in 1912, proved unsatisfactory for technical reasons and the easy-to-remember dashes and dots that coincidentally spell out *SOS* were retained. *Mayday*, not *SOS*, is the *oral* radio signal for requesting aid and probably derives from the French *"M'aidez*, "help me."

Soul Ships

In Brittany, up until the late nineteenth century, *soul ships* were believed to sail to the Bay of Souls near Point du Ray and collect recently deceased sailors for the journey to the fabled "Isles of the Blessed" somewhere to the west. These *soul ships* were sighted by many a mariner, just as mermaids and sea serpents were.

Sounding, Sound

The *sounding* that determines the depth of the water by means of a line and lead is of no relation to the word *sound*, meaning something audible, which derives from the Latin *sonus. Sounding* comes from the Old English word *sund*, for "water, sea, or swimming." The *sound* that is an inlet of the sea has the same roots.

Spencer Jacket

George John, the second Earl of Spencer and first Lord of the British Admiralty, who early recognized Lord Nelson's potential, created this short wool jacket that bears his name. Another Spencer, possibly related, invented the *Spencer sail*, and still another, the cork-filled *Spencer life belt.*

Spinnaker
In the 1860s an unknown yacht owner invented a sail rigged at right angles from his racing vessel's side, a sail that extended from mast-head to deck and ballooned far out to take advantage of the slightest breeze. The racing vessel was named *Sphinx*, but its crew had diffi-culty in pronouncing its name, calling it *Spinnicks.* Thus, the new sail was referred to as *Spinnicker's sail* and finally became known as a *spinnaker.* At any rate, no better explanation has been offered for the word.

Spit and Polish
As anyone who has served in the armed forces would suspect, the term is military in origin. It goes back to Victorian times, probably to the middle of the nineteenth century, although it isn't recorded be-fore 1895. Meticulous cleaning and smartness of appearance were demanded of sailors in the Victorian Navy, which became known as the "Spit-and-Polish Navy." Enlisted men liked it then no more than they do now and *spit and polish*—the application of one's spittle as a polishing agent and much elbow grease to make an object shine— came to be a pejorative term for such finicky, wasteful work in general.

Splice the Main Brace; Mainstay
No one knows exactly why *splice the main brace* has come to mean taking a strong, intoxicating drink. The main brace on a ship is the line secured to the main yard, from which the mainsail flies. The implication might be that a good drink braces one. However, one authority says the term derives from the days of sail, when the main brace was the most difficult to splice, being in a highly dangerous position, and that the crew received a double tot of rum after finish-ing the job on it. The first recorded use of *mainstay* as "one's chief support" is by Thomas Jefferson in 1787. This term derives from the important stay or thick rope that secures a sailing ship's mainmast forward.

The Spoils of the Conquered Ocean
Deciding to become conqueror of Britain in A.D. 40, the mad Roman emperor Caligula, who had made his horse Incitatus a priest and a consul of Rome, started to move his legions across the Channel from Gaul. Then he suddenly changed his mind and took his men on a march up and down the beach hunting for seashells! According to the Roman historian Suetonius, when Caligula's legions gathered enough shells, the emperor marched them home in self-acclaimed triumph carrying "the spoils of the conquered ocean."

To Stand Aloof
The expression *stand aloof* was originally a sea term meaning to luff, or bear to windward, deriving from the Dutch *loef*, "windward." Since it meant to keep to the windward and this cannot be done except by heading the ship away, *to stand aloof* came to mean to keep away from, to be standoffish.

To Stand the Gaff, Gaff
To stand the gaff means to endure goading or kidding by someone. Its nautical roots extend to the Provençal word *gaf* for a boathook. *Gaff* for a hoax or trick possibly derives from the idea of "hooking some poor fish," from the time when a large fishhook was referred to as a gaff.

The Standing Fishes Bible
Through the years various editions of the Bible have earned popular names because of printers' errors. In the so-called Standing Fishes Bible (1806), Ezekiel, 48:10, reads: "And it shall come to pass that the fishes [instead of *fishers*] shall stand upon it. . . ."

Starboard, Larboard
Stars in heaven have nothing to do with *starboard.* Old English ships were steered *(steor,* "steer") by a paddle or board *(bord)* over the right side. This *steorbord* later became *starboard* and *starboard* then became the name for the right side of the ship itself. *Larboard,* the left side of a ship, derives from the earlier *lureboard* (from the

Anglo-Saxon *laere*, "empty"), in reference to the fact that the left side was usually empty because the steersman stood on the right, or steering-board (*starboard*), side.

"The Star-Spangled Banner"

"The *Star-Spangled Banner*," written aboard ship by Francis Scott Key in 1814, did not become our national anthem until 1931, when Congress made it so by law. Although Key wrote the words during a naval battle against the British during the War of 1812, the music, ironically enough, was lifted from the official song of a London Masonic club entitled "To Anacreon in Heaven."

Statue of Liberty

> Not like the brazen giant of Greek fame,
> With conquering limbs astride from land to land,
> Here at our sea-washed, sunset gates shall stand
> A mighty woman with a torch, whose flame
> Is the imprisoned lightning, and her name
> Mother of exiles. From her beacon-hand
> Glows world-wide welcome; her mild eyes command
> "Keep ancient lands, your storied pomp!" cries she
> With silent lips,
> "Give me your tired, your poor,
> Your huddled masses yearning to breathe free,
> The wretched refuse of your teeming shore,
> Send these, the homeless, tempest-tossed to me:
> I lift my lamp beside the golden door.

So reads Emma Lazarus's famous sonnet engraved on a plaque inside the pedestal of the statue of Liberty Enlightening the World, as it is officially entitled. The Statue of Libery is, of course, as much a symbol of the United States as Uncle Sam. The colossal structure at the entrance to New York Harbor was a gift from France to the United States designed by French sculptor Frédéric Auguste Bartholdi; its steel framework was designed by Gustave Eiffel, designer of the Eiffel Tower. French citizens contributed the $250,000 for the statue itself and Americans gave $250,000 for its pedestal on Bed-

*One of the first drawings of the Statue of Liberty released
to the public*

An old print shows the Clermont, *"Fulton's Folly," departing on her first voyage*

loe's Island, whose name changed in 1956 to Liberty Island. Dedicated in 1886, the statue is now under the protection of the National Park Service, which administrates it along with Ellis Island, a former detention center for immigrants entering America, as part of the Statue of Liberty National Memorial. In the statue's left arm is a tablet with the date July 4, 1776, engraved upon it. At its feet are the broken shackles of tyranny.

Steamboat, Fulton's Folly

Steamboat is an Americanism dating back to at least 1785, when John Fitch invented the first workable one. Fitch was not able to secure the financial aid necessary to promote his invention after his fourth ship was destroyed and died a broken man, leaving a request that he be buried on the banks of the Ohio River so that he might rest "where the song of the boatman would enliven the stillness of my resting place and the music of the steam engine soothe my spirit." His dream became a reality in 1807, nine years after he died, when Robert Fulton's steamboat *Clermont*, which had been called "Fulton's Folly," proved a great success.

Steerage

One often hears the expression "My grandparents came over in steerage" in reference to late nineteenth-century immigrants to America. What the word means is passage belowdecks near a ship's steering gear. Steerage passage in the late nineteenth century cost only fifteen dollars. This price, plus twenty-five dollars to prove you weren't a pauper, was all one needed to come to America.

From Stem to Stern

Since the *stem* is, loosely speaking, the bow of a ship and the *stern* is the rear, the expression *from stem to stern* means "throughout," as in, "We turned the place over *from stem to stern*." The expression is an ancient one, dating back to at least the early sixteenth century.

Stepping the Mast

When a mast is about to be *stepped*, all those on board the new ship contribute good-luck coins to be placed under it. This old maritime tradition is said to have its origins in the ancient Roman custom of placing coins in the mouths of men killed in battle. The coins were supposed to pay Charon, the mythical ferryman, for transporting the dead man across the River Styx. Today the coins are often placed in corrosionproof receptacles at the base of the mast and the mast is *stepped*, or put in place, immediately afterward.

Stinkpots

Stinkpots were favorite weapons of pirates. They were maladorous concoctions made from saltpeter (potassium nitrate), limestone (calcium carbonate), asafetida (a vile-smelling gum resin) and decayed fish that were packed into earthenware jugs, ignited and hurled onto an enemy ship. Nauseating smoke spread over the deck and through the hold, often discouraging the enemy from fighting, or at least weakening his resistance. Pirates also suspended stinkpots from the yardarms and cut them off when they projected over the vessel under attack.

To Strike Sail; Labor Strike

When a nineteenth-century sailing ship engaged in combat let down her topsails at least mainmast high, she was said to *strike*, or "submit" to the ship she was fighting. Thus *to strike sail* came to mean to acknowledge one's defeat, "to eat humble pie." When in 1758 British sailors threatened to strike the sails on their ships and cease work unless their grievances were settled, our word for a labor *strike* was born.

Supreme Example of Allied Confusion

This was a World War II American and British term, originating with American sailors, that was a sarcastic play on the initials SEAC, which stood for the *S*outh *E*ast *A*sia *C*ommand.

Swabbie

Swab was used in the eighteenth century to mean a merchant seaman, probably deriving from the Dutch *swabbe*, "mop," in reference to sailors swabbing or mopping the decks. As far back as 1592, sailors who cleaned the decks were called *swabbers*. *Swabbie*, related to both these terms, came into use in the late nineteenth century and was used by Herman Melville in *White-Jacket.*

Swashbuckler

Today a *swashbuckler* is the name for an action-packed, romantic film or novel featuring much swordplay, especially one about pirates. The word, in its oldest sense, means a swaggering show-off and was used this way in Elizabethan times. A *buckler* was a small shield used to catch the sword blows of an opponent and to *swash* meant to dash against. *Swashbucklers* apparently dashed or banged their own shields a lot prior to a fight, or while they walked through the streets, but weren't always good swordsmen. They also had a reputation for taking money to defend someone and running when the going got tough.

192

Switchel

Switchel is old Yankee sailors' slang for a very thirst-quenching drink of molasses and water seasoned with vinegar and ginger. But I've seen the word used in contexts where it had to be an *alcoholic* drink, as in Jeremiah N. Reynold's 1835 account of a whale hunt for Mocha Dick, the prototype of Herman Melville's Moby-Dick. Therefore, *switchel* almost surely was commonly seasoned with rum, as several writers suggest. Unfortunately, the origin of the word, first recorded in a 1700 poem by Philip Freneau, is unknown, but here is a spiritless recipe: Mix together 1 gallon water, 2 cups sugar, 1 cup molasses, 1 cup vinegar, 1 teaspoon ginger and "hang in the well to cool." Add what you want to make it spirituous.

Tadpole, Toady

Tade was an early spelling for *toad*, and *pol* meant "head" in seventeenth-century speech. Therefore, *tadpole* means "toad head," an appropriate name for the early stage of a toad or frog when it is little more than a big head with a small tail. The synonym *polliwog* comes from *pol*, "head," and *wiglen*, "to wiggle" (later corrupted in speech to *wog*), meaning "wiggle head." As for *toady*, it dates back to the seventeenth century, when audiences would oooh and ahhh after helpers of traveling medicine men ate toad legs and the charlatans promptly "cured" them with some worthless tonic that was then sold to the onlookers. These assistants became known as *toad eaters*, and seemed so fawning—to the extent of eating "poisonous creatures" for their masters!—that their name in the corrupted form of *toady* became the word for a totally subservient person.

Take Down a Peg

In Elizabethan England a ship's colors were raised and lowered by a system of pegs; the higher the peg, the higher the honor. Colors that were taken down a peg, therefore, reduced the esteem in which the ship was held, even by its crew. This practice probably suggested the expression *to take down a peg*, to humble someone, lower him in his own or everyone else's eyes, which dates back to about the same time. The phrase might have been suggested by some early games where pegs were used for scoring, but no evidence of such a game has been found.

To Take the Wind out of His Sails

Here is an expression deriving from the nautical practice of sailing

A sailor getting a tattoo on South Street in New York City, about 1890
VALENTINE'S MANUAL OF OLD NEW YORK, *1896*

to the windward of another ship, thereby robbing its sails of the wind. Over the years the words came to mean to forestall or beat someone by using his own methods or material, to steal his thunder.

Tattoo
Captain James Cook was the first European to record the practice of *tattooing*, when he sailed the *Endeavor* on his historic exploration of the South Seas in 1769. Noting that the Tahitians cut their skin and injected a black dye that left a permanent mark when the wound healed, he called the practice *tattowing* in his diary. This was a fair approximation of the native word *tatau* for the operation. Within a short time the word was being spelled *tattoo.*

Tell It to the Marines

The British Royal Marines, formed in the eighteenth century, are the gullible ones here, not the U.S. Marine Corps. The Royal Marines, quartered aboard ships and responsible for discipline, among other duties, weren't well liked by sailors, who considered them stupid and gullible about the seafaring life and made them the butt of many jokes. Seamen even called empty bottles "marines." Any tall tale told to a sailor was likely to be met with the response "Tell it to the Marines—sailors won't believe it"; that is, sailors, unlike Marines, were too intelligent to believe it. The saying soon passed into popular use and was first recorded by Lord Byron in *The Island* (1823), Byron noting that it was an old saying even then.

A Tempest in a Teapot

Originally this saying for making a big fuss over a trifle was a *tempest in a teacup*. It has only been traced back to 1857, but is probably older. Similar early English sayings were "storm in a wash basin" and "a storm in a cream bowl" (1678). For that matter Cicero, as far back as 400 B.C., referred to a contemporary who "stirred up waves in a wine ladle," and he indicated that the expression was an old one.

Thames River, Set the Thames on Fire

England's Thames River, that cradle of so many far-flung sea expeditions, is usually pronounced to rhyme with *hems*, not *James*. The name is first recorded as *Tamesis*, circa A.D 893. *To set the Thames on fire* is an old expression, said of the Rhine and other rivers as well, meaning to do something marvelous or to work wonders, to *almost set the world on fire*.

There's a Dead Cat on the Line

Researchers for the forthcoming *Dictionary of American Regional English* found twenty-one people who used this expression, meaning there's something suspicious, something wrong, but not one of them could explain it. When William Safire asked readers of his nationally syndicated word column for help, an old man in Louisiana scrawled a letter explaining that the expression has its roots in fishing for catfish, when trotlines with many hooks on them are set in the water. The lines are checked every day, so if a fisherman checks a neighbor's line and *there's a dead catfish* (cat) *on the line*, he knows there's something wrong, something suspicious or fishy going on.

Three Sheets to the Wind

"Sheets" are not sails in nautical use, as many landlubbers believe. Neither are they bed coverings. A *sheet* is the rope or chain attached to the lower corner of a sail that is used for shortening or extending it. When all three *sheets* on a sailing ship are loosened, allowed to run free, the sails flap and flutter in the wind without restraint and the ship reels and staggers like a drunken person. Thus sailors would say a person slightly drunk had *one sheet to the wind* and that someone who could barely navigate had *three sheets to the wind.* The expression is first recorded in Pierce Egan's *Life in London* (1821) and then in Richard Henry Dana's *Two Years Before the Mast* (1840).

To Throw Cold Water On (Something), Hydrotherapy

To "cold-pie" or "cold-pig" someone, to wake him up by throwing cold water on him, was a practice well known and despised in Elizabethan times. Perhaps cold-pigging suggested the expression *to throw cold water on* (something), to discourage a plan or practice, for it surely ruined many a good dream. But a lot of guesses are possible here. The expression is at least two hundred years old and could also have been suggested by *hydrotherapy*, the so-called ocean "cold water cures" with which many a physical and mental illness was treated by dousing a patient with cold seawater. Anyway, the treatment was said to reduce the "mental heat" of extremely nervous persons and make them apathetic. The Cold-Bath Fields established in 1697, a district near London, was famous for this treatment.

Tide

A sea tide is usually thought to be high or low water, anything between ebb and flood, but *tide* really means "the fixed time of flood and ebb." *Tide* was originally a synonym for *time*, so the expression "Time and tide wait for no man" is something of a tautology.

Tin Cans

American destroyers were called *tin cans* during World War II because they were our smallest, thinnest-armored fleet vessels. They were also called "rust buckets" at the time, though "rust bucket" more often meant any old ship.

Tobit's Fish

Tobit, the principal character in the Book of Tobit, included in the Old Testament Apocrypha, was blinded by the dung of sparrows while he slept in a courtyard. The angel Raphael bid Tobit's son to catch a huge fish in the Tigris and apply its gall to Tobit's eyes, thus curing him of his blindness.

Torpedo

The electric ray, or torpedo fish, was the first *torpedo*, taking its name from the Latin *torpere*, "to be stiff or numb," in reference to the ray's numbing sting. In World War I, naval men named the self-propelled mines called *torpedoes* after the fish because the mines resembled the actions of the electric ray, stunning all that came into contact with them. Yet *torpedo* meant a percussion shell before this, in 1786, and described a stationary explosive mine, the kind Admiral Farragut spoke of when he said, "Damn the torpedoes, full speed ahead!" The torpedoes Farragut disdained, were in fact, beer kegs filled with powder.

Torpedo Juice

In World War II thirsty sailors sometimes made a potent drink called *torpedo juice* from alcohol drained from Navy torpedoes. This deadly brew soon lent its name to any raw homemade whiskey with killing power.

Touch and Go

Either ship pilotage or coach driving gave us this term for a narrow escape or a precarious situation in which the outcome is doubtful for a brief time. Coach drivers used the term *touch and go* for a narrow escape after the wheels of two coaches touched in a near accident, a favorite scene in many costume adventures. *The Sailor's Word Book* (1867) explains the term's possible nautical derivation: "Touch and go—said of anything within an ace of ruin; as in rounding a ship very narrowly to escape rocks, etc., or when, under sail, she rubs against the ground with her keel."

The children's game *touch and go*, similar to hide-and-seek, probably has no bearing on the phrase.

A Touch of Caruso

A lighthearted man of boyish charm and the greatest of tenors, Enrico Caruso (1873–1921) was something of a cutup and once pinched a girl's derriere in a Paris park. The resulting publicity gave rise to the expression *a touch of Caruso*, "Give her a touch of Caruso, chief!," meaning the turn of a ship's engines astern.

Trims His Sails

Though a sailor who *trims his sails*, taking advantage of the prevailing winds, is a good one, this nineteenth-century expression is usually applied to an opportunist in everyday life, one who is skillful in shifting his principles with the prevailing winds, without regard for anyone else.

Trolling

Trolling has nothing to do with the trolls or dwarfs of Scandinavian mythology. Meaning in its nautical sense to angle with a running line (which may have originally run on a *troll* or winch), or to trail a baited line behind a boat, the word *troll* has its beginnings in a hunting term, the Middle French *troller*, which meant "to go in quest of game," or "to ramble."

Trudgen Stroke

John Arthur Trudgen (1852–1902), an outstanding British amateur swimmer, introduced the *Trudgen stroke* to Europe in 1893, after seeing it used in South America. The stroke, employing a double overarm motion and a scissors kick, is regarded as the first successful above-water arm action used in swimming. Trudgen popularized the idea of minimizing water resistance by bringing both arms out of the water, which paved the way for the reception of the now common Australian crawl adopted from South Sea natives. His stroke was sometimes called the *Trudgeon*, a misspelling of the swimmer's name.

Tsunami

One of the few words in English of Japanese origin, *tsunami* means "storm wave" in that language. *Tsunami (soo-nam-ee)* waves have killed tens of thousands in recorded history. Starting as the result of an undersea volcanic eruption or earthquake, *tsunamis* gather force and can travel at over 400 miles an hour, rising to heights of over one hundred feet before they crash into shore. Though *tsunamis* have been traced back almost to the beginning of recorded history, the word itself did not come into English until the twentieth century.

Trolling was often done with drop lines in the 1860s
Smithsonian Institution

To Turn Turtle

British sailors in the Caribbean during the seventeenth century noticed that natives would capture huge sea turtles by turning them over, thereby rendering them helpless when the creatures came ashore to bury their eggs. Later they used this image when they said that a capsized ship had *turned turtle* and soon the expression came to mean anything upside down.

Twenty-one Gun Salute

A *twenty-one gun salute* is an American expression, but guns were fired as salutes in the early days of the British Navy. Says an official U.S. Navy publication:

Guns could not be loaded quickly then, so the act of firing one in a salute indicated that the saluter had disarmed himself

At the time when the Trudgen stroke was invented, bathers did their swimming from a bathhouse on wheels pulled out to sea by horses

LIBRARY OF CONGRESS

in deference to the person being saluted. The larger the number of guns fired, the greater degree of disarmament. . . .

Since twenty-one guns was the number found on one side of one of the larger ships of the line, firing all of them became the highest mark of respect, reserved for heads of state. Smaller numbers of guns were fired in salutes to people of lesser importance. But for salutes only odd numbers are used, reflecting the old seagoing superstition against even numbers. This form of saluting was first recognized in the U.S. in 1875. As Commander-in-Chief, the President is accorded the highest salute of twenty-one guns.

U-boat, Sub

David Bushnell's 1775 "Bushnell's *American turtle*" wasn't called a *U-boat*, even though it was America's first undersea *boat*. The term *U-boat* was coined in the 1890s, while submarines have only been called *subs* since about 1914. Like Bushnell's, regular U.S. Navy submarines are still named after fish and other marine creatures, though ballistic missile submarines are named for American heroes.

Unusual Nautical Names

Pearl Harbor . . . Evan Keel . . . Felonious Fish . . . Halibut Justa Fish . . . even a Commander Sink, U.S.N. . . . . These are just a few of the nutty names of real people noted in John Train's *Even More Remarkable Names* (1979). They are the only "nautical names" I came upon in Mr. Train's book, but they provide a good starting point for anyone who wants to make a collection of unusual real names relating to the sea.

Up Periscope!

First used by the English on land to see over hills and bushes, its use recorded as early as 1822, the *periscope* became forever linked with submarines during World War I. At the time, "up periscope!" became a familiar command and *feather* became the word for a periscope's wake. The word *periscope* itself is a learned coinage from the Greek *peri*, "near," and *scope*, "an instrument for observing."

Up the Creek

In a bad predicament, on the spot, behind the eight ball. Sometimes the expression is *up Salt Creek*, or even *up Shit Creek*—often *without a paddle.* The expression goes back about a hundred years and was probably first *up Salt Creek*, if we are to judge by the popular 1884 political campaign song "Blaine up Salt Creek." A salt creek is a creek leading through the salt marsh or marshland to the ocean and best explains the phrase, for it is very easy to get stuck in one and, without a paddle, a boatman would have no way to pole his way out. The excremental version conveys the same idea but makes the situation even worse.

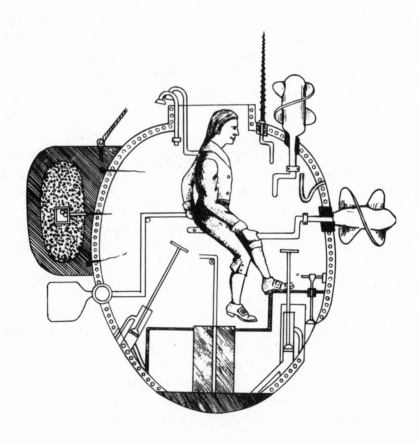

An old print shows "Bushnell's turtle," a submarine invented by David Bushnell and used in the Revolutionary War

"Use Him as Though You Loved Him"

It isn't true that Izaac Walton said of the worm, as bait for fish: "Use him as though you loved him, that is harm him as little as you may possibly, that he may live the longer." He was referring to the frog when he wrote this in his classic *The Compleat Angler, or the Contemplative Man's Recreation* but his words became misinterpreted over the years, probably because fishermen use worms more than frogs.

Vancouver

Vancouver, the largest city and chief port in British Columbia, *Vancouver* Island, the largest island off the west coast of North America, and the city of *Vancouver*, Washington, are all named for English navigator and explorer George Vancouver (1757–1798). Captain Vancouver, who sailed with Captain James Cook on his second and third voyages, explored and surveyed the northwest coast of America aboard *Discovery* in 1792. *Vancouver Island*, which he circumnavigated, was named in his honor at the time; *Vancouver*, Washington, was named directly from *Fort Vancouver*, founded by the Hudson Bay Company in 1825; and *Vancouver*, B.C., honored the explorer when it was incorporated in 1886. *Puget Sound* is named for Vancouver's Lieutenant Peter Puget, who helped the captain's brother finish his book, *A Voyage of Discovery to the North Pacific Ocean and Round the World* (1798). Vancouver died prematurely at the age of forty-one. *Vancouveria*, a small genus of low-growing evergreen shrubs belonging to the barberry family, also remembers the explorer. The shrubs are native to western North America.

Venus mercenaria

Clams, like many seafoods, are often regarded as a potent aphrodisiac, especially the common hard-shell clam *Venus mercenaria*. This quahog gets its last name from the Indian wampum beads used in commerce. It probably boasts its suggestive first name because Venus has often been depicted standing in a large seashell. A good example is Sandro Botticelli's famed "The Birth of Venus," sometimes jocularly called "Venus on the Half Shell."

The Vikings often used their open boats as dwellings while making raids ashore, when they took down the sails and covered the craft with them

Viking

From the eighth to the tenth century, the Scandinavian pirates who plundered the northern and western coasts of Europe were so dreaded that prayers began with "Lord, protect us from the Vikings. . . ." Their name is said to derive from the Old English *vicing*, "pirate," although this etymology is disputed and some experts hold that *Viking* comes from the Old English *wic*, "camp," because these Scandinavians set up temporary camps while carrying out raiding expeditions. Today *viking*, with a small *v*, can mean any sea-roving pirate or bandit.

Walk the Chalk

As early as the seventeenth century it was customary in the American navy for a straight line to be drawn with chalk along the deck of a ship as a test for drunkenness. Any sailor who couldn't walk the whole line, placing each foot on it, was adjudged drunk and punished accordingly—often by flogging. Thus, to *walk the chalk*, first recorded in 1823, came to mean walk a line of sobriety, to obey the rules.

Walk the Plank

No pirate ever forced anyone to *walk the plank* into the ocean—except in swashbuckling books and movies. Anyway, there is no authenticated record of real pirates employing a plank to dispatch their prisoners. Though Barbados pirate Major Stede Bonnet is reputed to have originated the cruel method of killing, no proof at all exists of the practice. There may have been an unrecorded, isolated instance of a blindfold prisoner walking the plank into a shark-infested sea, but it could not have been a common punishment and it most likely originated in the yarn of an old salt or from the pen of a nineteenth-century magazine illustrator. Pirates did feed captives to the fishes or told them they were free to "walk home" while far out at sea, but no planks were used. The common practice was to maroon prisoners and pirate offenders on a desert island. The offenders were simply put ashore naked, without any clothes or provisions.

The War of Jenkins's Ear

Bringing his left ear back to London in a leather case, master mariner Robert Jenkins claimed that Spanish sailors boarded his brig, the *Rebecca*, which had been peacefully trading in the West Indies, rifled her, and that their commander had lopped off the ear as a further humiliation. Jenkins sent his ear to the king and brought the matter before Parliament, which decided that this was one cutting Spanish insult too many. Jenkins's ear became the major cause of the war between England and Spain that led to the War of the Austrian Succession. The conflict, in 1739, was popularly called *the War of Jenkins's Ear*, which is definitely the oddest named of all wars and surely the only one ever initiated by an ear. Admiral Sir Edward Vernon (see Grog) put down the Spaniards at Portobelo and "One-Eared" Jenkins was given command of another ship in the East India Company's service. He later rose to company supervisor.

There is no evidence that pirates made captives walk the plank, as they are shown doing in this old print
THE PIRATE'S OWN BOOK, *1842*

To Warm the Cockles of One's Heart

The most popular explanation for the *cockles* in this expression—
most popular probably because it is the best story—says that late-
seventeenth-century anatomists noticed the resemblance of the
shape of cockleshells, the valves of a scalloplike mollusk, to the ven-
tricles of the heart and referred to the latter as *cockles*. Whether this
is the case or not, *cockles* isn't used much anymore except in the
expression *to warm the cockles of one's heart*, to please someone
immensely, to evoke a flow of pleasure or a feeling of affection. Behind the expression is the old poetical belief that the heart is the
seat of affection.

Water Phrases

A man for all waters: A Jack of all trades, well rounded
In deep water: In trouble
In low water: In financial trouble
In smooth water: In good circumstances
Still waters run deep: Someone quiet on the outside is more
worthwhile or dangerous than a big mouth.
That won't hold water: An argument that is wrong, that is a
vessel which leaks
To back water: To go easy and retrace one's steps, as in row-
ing a boat backward
To carry water to the sea: To carry coals to Newcastle
To fish in troubled water: (see page 71)

The Water Poet, Waterman

English poet John Taylor (1580–1653) was known as *the Water Poet*
because of the nature of many of his poems and the fact that he was
a river *waterman*, a boatman who transported passengers along the
River Thames. He claimed that he knew no grammar, though he had
written over eighty books.

Weather Rhymes

> Rainbow at night is the sailor's delight;
> Rainbow at morning, sailors, take warning.

Old salts are often able to predict the weather—and thus survive at sea—by observing the appearance of the sky, the direction of the wind, cloud formations and other natural phenomena. The following weather rhymes or jingles have for centuries helped mariners to remember these conditions.

> Mackeral skies and mares' tails
> Make tall ships carry short sails.

> July, stand by
> August, you must
> September, remember
> October, all over

> —*Rhyme to remember the seasons of West Indian hurricanes*

> When the porpoise jumps
> Stand by your pumps.

> With the rain before the wind
> Stays and topsails you must mind,
> But with the wind before the rain
> Your topsails you may set again.

> Seagull, seagull, sit on the sand,
> It's never good weather when you're on the land.

Weigh Anchor

The *weigh* in this phrase derives from the Old English *wegan*, "to carry or move," which later came to mean "lift" as well. Thus the expression means to lift or haul up the anchor. It is more correct, however, to say *under way* than *under weigh* to describe a ship in motion.

A Wet One, a Wet Ship

A wet one was in sailors' talk a vessel liable to ship water over the bow or gunwale. Wrote Captain Frederick Marryat in *Newton Fortes or the Naval Service* (1832): "She was what sailors term rather *a wet one*, and the sea broke continually over her bows." A *wet ship* is British naval slang for a ship that has a reputation for heavy drinking aboard.

Wetting a Commission

This old naval custom, dating back over a century, consisted of giving a party to a naval officer who had just received his commission. The parchment commission was formed into a cornucopia, filled with champagne and drunk from as it was passed from hand to hand.

White Cliffs of Dover

The *white cliffs of Dover* only became white when a huge white ship the size of a mountain tried to pass through the Strait of Dover and scraped the cliffs that color in its passage, according to ancient legend. Scientists have ruined a good story by establishing that the formation of the famous cliffs is due to the Foraminifera plankton.

The White Fleet

In 1907 the United States decided to show the world we were a great naval power by sending sixteen battleships and four destroyers on a world cruise. Because all these ships were painted white, they were popularly called the *White Fleet* or *Great White Fleet*.

Widow Maker

Rudyard Kipling is the first recorded writer to use *widow maker* as a synonym for the sea, in *Puck of Pook's Hill* (1906): "What is a woman that you forsake her. . . . To go with the old grey Widow-maker?"

Widow maker was used by Shakespeare for a killer in general, however, and it seems likely that the term was used before Kipling to describe the great elementary force that made widows of so many sailors' wives.

Widow's Walk, Captain's Walk

A *widow's walk* is an elevated observatory on a dwelling, often with a railing and affording a good view of the ocean. These watchtowers, often seen on the roofs of old dwellings, date back to Colonial times and were so named because many women walked in vain on them, waiting for incoming ships that never came home. Taking the form of a cupola or railed-in deck or balcony, they have also been called, less poetically, *the walk, the captain's walk, the observatory* or *the lookout.*

Winchester Geese

Prostitution and geese raising were two major Winchester industries in the sixteenth century and British prostitutes were called *Winchester geese* by sailors because they seemed almost as ubiquitous in the area as the birds. The first part of their name may honor the bishop of Winchester, however, as the brothels in Southwark were under his jurisdiction, and the Church received rent from many establishments based in houses he owned. These revenues, incidentally, helped found and maintain a number of esteemed Oxford colleges. A *Winchester goose* also came to mean a venereal bubo, or anyone infected with venereal disease.

Windjammer

A *windjammer* originally meant "a horn player," then came to mean a "talkative person or windbag," and finally, at the end of the nineteenth century, became the name for any ship with sails. It seems that windy defenders of sailing vessels at the beginning of the age of steamships boasted so much about the superiority of sail that they were called *windjammers* and their name soon became attached to the sailing ships they bragged about.

The Winds
The winds in Greek mythology were ruled by Aeolus, who kept them in a cave on Mount Haemus in Thrace. In one tale Aeolus gave Ulysses a bag tied with silver string in which all the unfavorable winds were stored, so that Ulysses might arrive home without delay by tempests. But Ulysses's crew opened the bag, believing it contained treasure, and their ship was driven off course back to Thrace. Ancient mariners believed such yarns about the winds and gave the winds their own special names, some of which are listed below.

North Wind: Boreas (Greek) or Aquilo (Latin)
South Wind: Notus (Greek) or Auster (Latin)
East Wind: Eurus (Greek)
West Wind: Zephyrus (Greek) or Favonius (Latin)
Northeast Wind: Argestes (Latin)
Northwest Wind: Corus (Latin)
Southeast Wind: Volturnus (Latin)
Southwest Wind: Ajerventus, Africus, Africanus or Libs (Latin)
North (but not due north) *Wind*:   Thrascias (Latin)
Trade Winds: Winds that regularly "blow trade" in one direction or another. In the Northern Hemisphere they blow from the northeast, and in the Southern Hemisphere from the southeast. In some places they blow six months of the year in one direction and six months in the opposite.

Windy Cap
Laplanders of yore and many other ancient people made a profitable trade in selling favorable winds to mariners, as did individuals like Bessie Millie of the Orkney Islands, who sold winds to sailors for sixpence as late as 1814. These people undoubtedly had knowledge of the weather that others didn't have at the time, but the belief persisted that they could influence the winds. It is said that King Eric of Sweden was so familiar with the evil spirits that controlled the winds that wherever he turned his cap, the wind would blow. Olaus Magnus, a Swedish historian, says he was commonly known as *Windy Cap*.

Women and Children First

For over a century this saying has been part of the unwritten law of the sea—women and children shall be saved before anyone else in the event of a disaster—and in the vast majority of cases, the words have been gallantly honored. The saying seems to have arisen, anonymously, after H.M.S. *Birkenhead* went down off the Cape of Good Hope in 1852 and 491 men were lost while all the women and children aboard were saved and a great tradition was born. There have, unfortunately, been cases of *women and children last* at sea, too, though they have been very few in comparison. On April 1, 1873, the British steamer *Atlantic* went down near Halifax, Nova Scotia. Over 560 lives were lost, including every woman aboard. Victorian morals and manners had been forgotten by the callous crew and genteel dandies aboard.

Despite the picture, a cowardly crew caused the death of all the women aboard the Atlantic, *when she sank in 1873*

LIBRARY OF CONGRESS

Wooden Walls

Ships of war were poetically named *wooden walls* because they were the wooden walls of England, keeping out invaders, in the days before the advent of ironclad ships.

Wouldn't Touch It with a Ten-Foot Pole

Why not a seven-foot pole or a nine-foot pole? The answer may be that the expression was suggested by the ten-foot poles that river boatmen used to pole their boats along in shallow waters, poles that were often cut ten-feet long. Possibly the expression was first something like *I wouldn't tough that with the ten-foot pole of a riverman* and that this shortened with the passing of pole boats from the American scene. However, the image first appears in the Nantucketism *can't touch him with a ten-foot*, meaning "he is distant, proud, reserved." In the sense of not wanting to get involved in a project or having a strong distaste for something, the words aren't recorded until the late nineteenth century.

Wreck of the Hesperus, *Norman's Woe*

A large submerged rock off the coast of Gloucester, Massachusetts, caused so many shipwrecks in the eighteenth century that it was called *Norman's woe*. Wrote Henry Wadsworth Longfellow in his diary for December 17, 1837: "News of shipwrecks horrible on the coast. 20 bodies washed ashore near Gloucester, one lashed to a piece of wreck. There is a reef called Norman's Woe where many of these took place; among others the schooner *Hesperus*. . . . I must write a ballad upon this." The ballad proved to be "The Wreck of the Hesperus," which began:

> It was the schooner *Hesperus*
> That sailed the wintry sea;
> And the skipper had taken his little daughter,
> To keep him company . . .

The poem became so well known that "wreck of the *Hesperus*" also became an expression for any disheveled thing, as in "You look like the wreck of the *Hesperus.*"

Wrens, Waves, Spars

Wrens, an acronym for the *W*omen's *R*oyal *N*aval *S*ervice, was coined in Great Britain during World War I and is the first acronym invented for a women's naval unit. The *Waves*, *W*omen *A*ccepted for *V*oluntary *S*ervice, seems more labored but worked during World War II. The most ingenious of such inventions is *Spar*, an acronym for the Woman's reserve of the U.S. Coast Guard Reserve (World War II), which was constructed from the Coast Guard motto: *S*emper *Para*tus, *A*lways *R*eady.

X-chaser

An *x-chaser* has been British naval slang for an officer with high qualifications, especially as to his scientific education, since about 1910. The *x* in the phrase is "the x which figures so disturbingly in mathematics," according to one authority on slang.

Xebec

A small three-masted vessel often used by pirates on the Mediterranean. Also called a *zebec* or *chebec* and deriving ultimately from the Arabic word *shabbak*, the vessel is today used to a small extent in commerce.

Xeme

The *Xeme* (pronounced *zem*) is the fork-tailed arctic gull familiar to maritime explorers and adventurers. It was first observed in Greenland by a British mariner in 1832.

XYZ Affair

President John Adams sent three representatives to France in 1797 to negotiate a maritime treaty that would prevent French pirates from attacking American ships. But three of Tallyrand's agents intercepted them and demanded a $1 million "loan" for France before they would be received by the French government. The agents refused to negotiate on these terms and returned home. One of them, Charles Cotesworth Pinckney, allegedly uttered the slogan "Millions for defense, sir, but not one cent for tribute." Pinckney, however, always claimed he only said: "No, no, no! Not a single sixpence!"

Yacht

This pleasure craft takes its name from a type of speedy German pirate ship of the sixteenth century called the *jacht* that was common on the North Sea. British royalty found that this type of vessel made excellent pleasure craft a century later, spelling the German word *yaught*, which finally became *yacht*.

A luxury liner towers over yachts in St. Thomas harbor
PRINCESS CRUISES

Yankee

The most popular of dozens of theories holds that *Yankee* comes from *Jan Kee* ("little John"), a Dutch expression the English used to signify "John Cheese" and contemptuously applied to Dutch seamen in the New World and then to New England sailors. From a pejorative nickname for New England sailors, the term *Jan Kee*, corrupted to *Yankee*, was applied to all New Englanders and then to all Americans during the Revolution; the most notable example of this is found in the derisive song *Yankee Doodle*. Nowadays, the British and others use *Yankee* for an American; southerners here use it for northerners, and northerners use it for New Englanders, who are usually proud of the designation.

Yardarm

A ship's *yard* (from the Anglo-Saxon *givid*) is a long, thin spar hung crosswise to the mast to support a square sail. The *yardarm* is simply one *arm* or part of this *yard*.

Yare

If memory serves me this term enjoyed some popularity twenty years or so ago in a Katharine Hepburn movie. In any case, *yare* (pronounced *yar*, which rhymes with *far*) has been around since the late fourteenth century as an expression for an easily manageable fine ship that answers readily to the helm. "Our ship is tyte and yare," Shakespeare wrote in *The Tempest*. Another famous literary use of the word occurs in Justin H. McCarthy's *A Ballad of Dead Ladies: After Villon, Envoy:*

> *Où sont les neiges d'antan?*
> Alas for lovers! Pair by pair
>   The wind has blown them all away;
> The young and yare, the fond and fair;
>   Where are the snows of yesterday?

In the poem *yare* is pronounced to rhyme with *fair*, as it sometimes is.

Yarn

"Come spin us a good yarn, father," Captain Marryat wrote in *Jacob Faithful* (1834). To *spin a yarn* was originally naval slang dating back to the early nineteenth century for "to tell a long, often incredible story." Its obvious source is the yarn lofts ashore where yarn was spun to supply ships with rope, work that took a long time and in which the threads of a rope were interwoven like the elements of a good story. Eventually *yarn* became a synonym for a story or tale itself.

Yoked

Yoked is today a synonym for "mugged." It arose with "Jumper Jacks," or muggers, who preyed on seamen, who *yoked* a sailor by grabbing him from behind by the yoke of his tight collar and twisting his neckerchief.

Zephyr

In naval parlance a *zephyr* is a soft, gentle breeze. It takes its name from Zephyrus, the Greek god of the west wind. Shakespeare makes the first recorded mention of the word in this sense in 1611: "They are as gentle as zephires blowing below the violet,/ Not wagging his sweet head."

Z-gram

While chief of U.S. Naval Operations, Admiral Elmo Zumwalt issued terse, direct memos that were models of conciseness and clarity. These were dubbed *Z-grams* and became naval slang for such model memos, a thing rare in the armed services.

Zigzag Course

A term that probably arose during World War I, a *zigzag course* is a ship's course first to the right of the base course and then to the left. It was originally used in avoiding enemy submarines, but the term is now applied to any devious action.

Zizz

Since at least 1930, *zizz* has meant "to sleep" in the British Navy because the word is suggestive of snoring. From this came the naval slang *zizzer* for "bed."

Zob

Zob is the name of an old game played among officers in the British Navy to decide which of two people will pay for drinks, but the custom is now known outside England and perhaps deserves greater currency. The players face one another, repeating the word *zob* three times. Each then makes either a closed fist, an open palm, or two fingers extended. The first of these signs "represents a stone, the open palm a sheet of paper, the fingers extended a pair of scissors." The game is decided on this basis: "Scissors can cut paper, stone can blunt scissors, and paper can wrap up a stone." Thus, a man who holds out two fingers (a scissors) beats a man who holds out an open palm (a piece of paper); a man who holds out a closed fist (a stone) beats a man who holds out two fingers (a scissors) et cetera. The man who loses two out of three *zobs* pays for the drinks.

Zyga; ZZ

For the next to last entry in our nautical word book we sail back to days of antiquity, when triremes and other vessels had cross-benches or thwarts for rowers called *zyga*. Each *zygon* held a number of rowers and varied in height depending upon the vessel. This may be interesting to know, but frankly it is included here because one would be hard put to find another nautical expression nearer the end of the alphabet, unless it was the symbol used for a *zigzag course* (see page 221), which is, and I hope this isn't putting any readers to sleep: *ZZ*.